KT-563-533

Contents

Acknowledgements   iv

Series Editor's Introduction by *Duncan B Forrester*   v

Walking in Darkness and Light   1

Hope in Times of Change: Four Biblical Reflections   7

Where there is no Peace   14

Carrying our own Crosses   19

Stand Firm   26

Sharing our Bread   32

Speak to Make a New World Possible   36

The Good News of Deliverance   43

Testimony Stoops to Mother Tongue   49

Faces of God   57

The Soft Whisper of a Voice   62

Speaking of Mary   70

After the War is Over   76

The Courage to Change   82

Acknowledgements

pp. 38–9 'Real' by Kathy Galloway, in *Struggles to Love* (London: SPCK, 1994, 1998).

p. 39 Rowan Williams, in *Resurrection* (London: DLT, 1982).

p. 40 From 'Eucharist Prayer for Good Friday' by Janet Morley, in *Bread of Tomorrow* (London: SPCK/Christian Aid, 1992).

p. 41 'The bodies of grownups' by Janet Morley, in *All Desires Known* (Women in Theology/Movement for the Ordination of Women, 1988, and SPCK [expanded edition, London, 1992]).

p. 56 'Spirit of truth …' by Janet Morley, in *All Desires Known* (Women in Theology/Movement for the Ordination of Women, 1988, and SPCK [expanded edition, London, 1992]).

p. 58 'Because She Cares' by Nancy Somerville, in *Pushing the Boat Out: New Poetry* ed. Kathy Galloway (Glasgow: Wild Goose Publications, 1995).

p. 59 'Credo' by Ruth Burgess, in *Pushing the Boat Out: New Poetry* ed. Kathy Galloway (Glasgow: Wild Goose Publications, 1995).

p. 61 'Lord, help us to see …' by Rubem Alves, Brazil, in *All Year Round* (BCC, 1987).

pp. 65, 66 From 'Auchinellan: Casting out the Demons', in *Talking to the Bones* by Kathy Galloway (London: SPCK, 1996).

p. 66 'I live on the edge' by Kay Carmichael, in *sweet, sour and serious* (Scotland: Survivors' Press, 1996).

ON REFLECTION SERIES

WALKING IN DARKNESS AND LIGHT

SERMONS AND REFLECTIONS

KATHY GALLOWAY

Series Editor:
Duncan B Forrester

SAINT ANDREW PRESS
EDINBURGH

First published in 2001 by
SAINT ANDREW PRESS
121 George Street, Edinburgh EH2 4YN

ISBN 0 7152 0769 5

British Library Cataloguing in Publication Data
A catalogue record for this book
is available from the British Library.

ISBN 0 7152 0769 5

Cover design by McColl Productions, Edinburgh

Printed and bound by Bell & Bain Ltd., Glasgow

Series Editor's Introduction

Duncan B Forrester

All down the ages Christians have reflected on their faith and its bearing on life. These reflections have taken a great variety of forms, but one of the most common has been the sermon. For generations notable preachers were well-known public figures, and books of sermons were a well-known literary genre. In many places people queued to hear great preachers, whose sermons were reported in the press, and discussed and dissected afterwards. Sermons launched great movements of mission, and revival, and social change. Sometimes influential preachers were imprisoned by the authorities so that their disturbing challenge should not be heard.

Nowhere was this tradition more lively than in Scotland. But today, some people say, the glory has departed. If you want to find great preaching today, the critics say, go to Africa, or Latin America, or to Black churches in the States. No longer in Scotland do people pack in their hundreds into huge churches to hear great preachers. The sermon seems to have lost its centrality in Scottish life. The conviction and the emotional surcharge that once sustained a great succession of notable preachers seems hard to find today. Has secularisation destroyed the appetite for sermons? Has the modern questioning of authority eroded the preaching office? Do Christians no longer reflect on their faith, or do they do it in other and newer ways?

This series of books shows that the tradition of preaching is still very much alive and well. It has changed, it is true, and it has adapted to new circumstances and new challenges. It is not the same as it was in the long afterglow of the Victorian pulpit. Reflection by the Scots on their faith, as these books illustrate, is perhaps more varied than it was in the past, and their sermons are briefer. But Scottish preaching is still passionate, thoughtful, biblical, challenging, and deeply concerned with the relevance of the gospel to the needs of today's world.

The reflections on the Christian faith in these books are challenging, disturbing, nourishing. They proclaim a Word that is alive and active, and penetrates to the depths of things, a Word that speaks of hope and worth, of forgiveness and new beginnings, of justice, peace and love. And so they invite the reader to engage afresh with the everlasting gospel.

Duncan B Forrester
EDINBURGH

ON REFLECTION ...

Other titles available in this series

Wrestle and Fight and Pray
John L Bell

Love Your Crooked Neighbour
Ron Ferguson

Laughter and Tears
James A Whyte

Go by the Book
Robert Davidson

Walking in Darkness and Light

(Isaiah 2, 1–5, Romans 13, 11–14)

One of the things about living in the city is that it never gets really dark. There's always a streetlight, a headlight, some neon, some window lit up probing into the shadows, casting a long glare into the night sky so it ceases to be black and glows instead with a kind of dull yellow glare. But I used to live on the Hebridean island of Iona, and *there* it was dark. Midnight on a moonless December night, not a star to be seen, or, even worse, 5am in February, no streetlights, no headlights, no friendly houses burning the night-time lamps – there I learned what it was like to walk in the dark.

Perhaps I would be going home from the Abbey, having, as usual, forgotten my torch, and, on a wide path that I walked a hundred times a week, which, in reality, I knew like the back of my hand, I'd be slipping and stumbling, tripping over my feet, splashing through puddles, missing the gate, and sometimes losing my way so badly that I ended up in the graveyard, scraping my knees as I fell over the gravestones.

Or I'd be observing the penitential rite of getting up to go somewhere on the early ferry on the winter timetable – Monday morning 5am – and I'd be going down the steep brae to the jetty in the absolute darkness that comes before the greyest of dawns, a dark, sleeping house behind me, a dark sea before me, an icy wind whipping round my frozen ears and a treacherous road between me and the ferry, which I couldn't see but knew was bound to be on its way because I'd left the house just a little too late. Somewhere to get to – and no light, none at all, not even a glimmer.

Perhaps because we so rarely experience real darkness, it's easy to forget what it's actually like to walk in the dark. Here are some of the things I remember about walking in the dark.

First, and most obviously, it takes you much longer to get where you're going, and sometimes you don't get there at all: you get lost, or you get fed-up or despondent, you turn back, you give up – you miss the ferry!

And then, you feel it in your body: not just in the shortened steps, the bruised shins as you bump into things, but also in the clenched jaw, in the tension across your shoulders that locks itself into you unconsciously, and in the constraints it places on your mobility. You can't run or wander about the road; it's hard to saunter in the dark.

You hear noises, and in the dark they seem different, louder, stranger, perhaps more threatening than they would in the day. Your imagination plays tricks on you, and fear rises. Your heart starts to race.

In the daylight, the road I was walking on is one of the most beautiful in Scotland. It overlooks a sea which is at the same time eternally restless and eternally restful, mountains, glowing red rock. Ditches full of wild flowers, lichens, pebbles and the dazzle of water. In the dark, you cannot see the beauty around you. Walking in the dark, you are guarded, tense, fearful. Freedom, mobility, beauty, relaxation are all gravely limited. I remember with what relief I would see the little pinpoint of light that was the ferry appear out of the darkness of the waves, because it meant that my walk in the dark was over.

It was with these vivid, powerful and contrasting memories of walking in darkness and light that I came to these two passages we've heard read this morning. The first is from the book of the prophet Isaiah, writing in the 8th century BC, almost 3000 years ago. He was writing at a time when the Israelites of Judah were being threatened by a powerful neighbour, the Assyrians, and through the first 39 chapters of Isaiah, the prophet is calling the people of Israel not only to an awareness of this threat, but to what he saw as a much graver threat, that of their own injustice and disobedience. Driven by the urgency of his message, agonised by their failure to pay any attention, this most poetic of all the prophets drew a stark picture of his people with their bloodstained hands, their pious platitudes, their wrong relationships and the judgements they would inevitably bring upon themselves. But this passage, also familiar to us from Isaiah's contemporary Micah, was probably a hymn of the temple, which does what Isaiah does again and again, which is to set the prophecy of judgement in a framework of hope. This devastation, he says, this ruin which you are bringing upon yourselves, is not the last word. There is hope for the future.

And it's a remarkable poem of hope, this vision of the nations streaming in, not now bent on conquest and oppression, but neither coming beaten, bowed and enslaved, but of their own free will, gladly, to find the paths that lead to peace, to settle their disputes, to beat their swords into ploughs, their weapons into tools for growth. *There will be no more war.* You can't help but *love* this vision, not just for then but for now, for Rwanda and the Congo and Kosovo and Ireland, and for all the war-torn, bloodstained places where people walk without freedom, without beauty, without mobility, without peace.

The Romans' passage too picks up the theme of the coming of the light. In the mystery religions of the Roman Empire in Paul's time, the idea of wakening from sleep was a common image for spiritual renewal and awakening, and it's clearly linked to the break of day and the rising of the sun. Paul is saying, why do you assume that the time of salvation is *not* now, *now* is when you have to live in the light.

So we have these two passages about the light, which both contain within them twin elements of hope and judgement, and I have my powerful memories of walking in darkness and light, and I am seeking to draw out the thread that connects them all for me on this first Sunday in Advent. So I will try to share with you what these passages and these memories are saying to me.

When I was a child, I used to love the first Sunday in Advent; for the lighting of the first candles on the Advent wreath, and for the hymn we will sing today, the 'Veni Emmanuel', O Come, o come Emmanuel, and for all these readings, which, I didn't know then but know now, were the great Isaiah texts. I loved them because they were a sign that something was coming, something was about to happen, some breakthrough was going to be made – and I don't think it was all just related to Santa Claus and Christmas presents and a baby in a manger, though that was certainly part of it. It was like something that was both going to happen any day, here, in my world, but was also something happening quite beyond or outside time. It was mysterious and huge and yet not very far from me at all. I don't think I ever found a religious song that expressed the feeling half so well as that one from *West Side Story,* which maybe you know, called 'Something's Coming':

> *... Could be, who knows, it's only just out of reach,*
> *down a block, on a beach, under a tree ...*

When I got a bit older, I thought the feeling was connected with the wonderful hopes and promises of Isaiah, for a world that always needed peace and justice and integrity, and wolves and sheep lying down together, and Advent was about the rebirth of these hopes in the midst of cynicism and apathy. It was about waiting for the coming of the light.

But now I know it wasn't waiting for the coming of the light. Now I know the light was always there ... before the world began ... beyond time and space, yet coming right down into the midst of my time and space. Isaiah knew the light was there, and he went half-demented struggling to get people to see it, one minute trying to show them the awful, constrained half-lives they were living, fearful, grabby, scarred by all the things they were always bumping into in the dark, stubbornly refusing to take the risk of joy and beauty and freedom, and the next minute with the vision of life in the light spilling out of him.

Paul knew the light was there too – no one knew it better than this wee, driven, bossy, complex character, plagued by ill-health and uncomprehending colleagues, yet ablaze with the light across continents, in prison, in constant danger, always trying to convince, to persuade, to lecture and argue and love his little flocks into the freedom of the light. You know, I look at the passage we read this morning, and my heart sinks, and I think, oh no, not another one of Paul's dreary lists of things not to do, which, even though I don't do most of them, set up an immediate conflict in me against the notions of 'oughts'. What is this? I'm getting angry at being asked not to do things I don't want to do anyway? No. What I'm reacting to is what seems like laying down the law! I am not much moved by orders, except possibly in fear.

We do Paul such an injustice by constantly turning him, of all people, into a moralist. I want to read back the three verses before the ones we read:

> Be under obligation to no one – the only obligation you have is to love one another. Whoever does this has obeyed the Law. The commandments, 'Do not commit adultery; do not murder; do not steal; do not desire what belongs to someone else' – all these, and any others beside, are summed up in the one command, 'Love your neighbour as you love yourself.' If you love someone, you will never do them wrong; to love, then, is to obey the whole Law.
> You must do this, because you know that the time has come for you to wake up from your sleep. For the moment when we will be saved is closer now than it was when we first believed.
> (Romans 13, 8–11)

Yes! This is what moves me; this is what I give my 'yes' to; this is not my duty but my desire. Legalism leaves me in darkness. But love brings me into the light.

To walk in the light is to walk freely not fearfully, to see and delight in all the beauty around us: in people, in nature, desiring it to be allowed to remain beautiful. It is to walk with a light heart, relaxed not tense, to have choices. The light is in the world. There is an old Jewish saying, 'Do not say, God is in my heart. Rather, say, I am in the heart of God.' The gospel of Jesus says precisely this thing. I am in God's heart, and you, and you and you. Loved, valued, unconditionally accepted, we live and move and have our being in the heart of God, which is the light of God.

But if this is so, why do we then choose to stumble around fearfully in the dark, cutting each other up? Why would you choose that, rather than freedom and justice and joy? Perhaps it's because if you live in the heart of God, you have to live from the inside out rather than the outside in. You have to leave behind the world of appearances and sensations and surfaces and exteriors and go in deeper. You have to go closer to the light. And in the light, we're so afraid our blemishes, our warts, our insecurities, our nasty little secrets and meannesses will show up. It's very hard to let go of the idea of judgement as our enemy and learn to see it as our friend. Of course, that's because we're basing our understanding on human judgement, which is partial, often hostile and self-seeking, and very much from the outside. God's judgement, however, is somewhat different. It forgives, heals, renews and sets free those who come near enough to feel it, like feeling the sun's rays. Artists do not paint in the dark; they seek the light on their work so that they can make it better work. They know judgement as their friend.

And the other thing about living in the heart of God is that from there, we have to let go of pride. We are not alone in God's heart. We are not even simply in company we'd approve of. Maybe it's not just Baptists and Presbyterians. Maybe it's not just law-abiding and socially well-adjusted citizens. Maybe it's the people we most disapprove of. Maybe in the light of God, there's not so much difference between us: human, flawed, interesting, lovable.

For myself, as I read along with Isaiah and Paul and the gospels throughout Advent, I will also be looking at the ways in which I stumble around in the darkness, living out of my fears rather than the freedom that has been given to me by the grace of God. And I will be remembering the words often used in the Iona Community, and which are so appropriate to the Advent season, *'Follow the light you have and pray for more light.'*

Hope in
Times of Change

Four Biblical Reflections

'They will become a nation'
(Genesis 21, 9–20)

Whenever I hear this story, it reminds me of the need to read the Bible not without reverence but with a measure of caution. Here is a woman without a land, uprooted, enslaved, removed from all that her land could offer her – the means of providing for her child, a place to belong, perhaps people to belong with. Like landless people everywhere, her rights have been taken away from her. Even the territory of her body has been invaded, colonised, plundered – and then abandoned, dumped in no-man's land.

The recorders of histories have a tendency to interpret them in their own interest, but with the best will in the world, and allowing for all the cultural and historical differences, Abraham does not come out of this story well. In the interests of justice, we need to hear the histories not part of history too. And it would be a travesty of justice to read this story as just an incident, however regrettable, in someone's personal religious drama. It's a political story too.

Of course, it predates the Jubilee teaching of Leviticus 25, of restoration of land, freedom from slavery and the cancellation of debts. And though Jubilee seems to have been mostly an ideal rather than a practice, even the ideal of it was unthinkable for Hagar. For her, there was only the desolation of landlessness, and of fearing to watch her child die.

And what of God in this story? We understand God to have

7

justified Abraham in his actions. Well, perhaps that depends on who you believe is the author of the story. There are a lot of people who have suffered under 'God told me to do it.'

But we also hear that God heard Hagar crying, and God's angel spoke to her … words of comfort … words of promise. Promise of survival first … but then that great promise that resounds through the whole of the Old Testament … *'you will become a nation'*. It is the promise to the Jews – but not just to the Jews – *'you will become a nation'*. They were communal times; there was no thought of salvation, of liberation, of hope for the future outside that promise. *'You will become a nation.'* A nation with a land.

We are familiar with that aspiration still; here in Scotland, we have taken a huge step in self-determination, and land reform in a land where 5% of the people own 80% of it is high on the agenda. But such aspirations are not so easily met in other places. *'You will become a nation'* could equally be said of the landless of the world – and a great nation it is, to be sure. Is there a Jubilee strategy of hope for them?

In the New Testament, the promise, the covenant has a different emphasis. Here, the nation is not one based on blood or kinship. There is no promised land. There is only the community of justice and love. Whatever the dispensation of the individual, justice and love are never individual, private matters. They are only possible in the context of the community. This is the meaning of the nation.

There is no mention in Genesis of God descending from heaven on a cloud and restoring Hagar to her land. I have no expectation of God doing it in the year 2000 either. My only hope is in the nation of justice and love, which, I should add, I have never found to be restricted to Christians alone. This nation of justice and love would seem to be the only community in which the desperate questions of land restoration and reclamation can be negotiated without another endless round of dispossession and slaughter.

It's easy to be cynical about such a community. However, I have taken a modest hope from the fact that in Scotland, the people, as well as voting overwhelmingly for a Scottish Parliament, also voted by a considerable majority for tax-varying powers, in effect, for the possibility of *higher* taxes. Conventional wisdom has it that individualistic, materialistic Westerners will *never* vote for higher taxes. Conventional wisdom is not always right. The nation of people across the world who still want to be part of the community of justice and love may be bigger than we think. Their struggle is more with how to effect change in the face of unaccountable institutions. Which takes us back to politics, and the need to strategise in ways that mobilise the nation of justice and love beyond the limitations of the nation state – surely an ecumenical task. A task for the great nation we represent beyond our individual nations.

'He cancelled the debts of both'
(Luke 7, 36–50)

Here is a rich and profound text from Luke's gospel. We begin with a respectable man, a moral man. He considers he knows the difference between right and wrong, and he is complaining about an incident that is in his view, unsuitable and unseemly, morally wrong.

Jesus sees that this man has a blindness, an attitude of the heart that prevents him from understanding the incident in the way that he, Jesus, understands it. So he tells him a story of two men who both owed money, who had debts they could not pay. One was a little debt; one was a huge debt. But the moneylender cancelled them both.

It would be a mistake to draw too close a parallel from this story of debt cancellation. The International Monetary Fund and the World Bank bear little resemblance to the moneylender, still less are they like the forgiving God of whom Jesus talks. And the cancellation of debt is not to be equated with the forgiveness of sins – in any case, today, the weight of injustice is tilted in the other direction.

Nevertheless, there is a deep truth here that has some relevance – about the attitude of the heart, the hardness which causes partial vision. We see our own self-righteousness, and it narrows our horizons, blinds us to another kind of reality. Jesus and the woman who anointed him saw each other with the eyes of love; it was a new way of seeing, and it opened up many possibilities, including the possibility of justice.

That melting of the hardened heart is the experience of grace, which comes when we are vulnerable, exposed, personal, not self-justifying. It expresses itself freely and extravagantly. If freedom is the ability to look another straight in the eye, unbound, then grace is a new way of seeing, with the eyes of love, which transforms our reality.

If we have anything different as Christians to bring to our life and work, it is surely this experience of grace, unconditional in its giving and receiving, as the context and reality, as the wider vision against which we measure our principles *and* our practice. It is this experience which binds us together in the *oecumene*, the household of faith, the community of those who see each other with the eyes of love.

'Not counting the women and children'
(Matthew 14, 13–31)

I love this story because it shows Jesus in his struggle for solitude and prayer, grieving for the death of his cousin John, and yet following the movement of his heart, going out in compassion to the people. And I love it for the bit that says, *'everyone ate, and had enough'*. It is, I think, one of the most beautiful lines in the Bible, this picture of sufficiency, of sharing – 'everyone ate, and had enough'.

But this story, presumably quite unconsciously for the writer, also demonstrates, simply and rather appallingly, two thousand years of a particular blindness of Christian history: *'the number who ate was about five thousand men, not counting the women and children'*. What a history of exclusion that sums up, of the people who are not counted, who have been, and continue to be, invisible in so many ways – in their poverty, in their unnoticed labour, in their wasted potential. It is an invisibility that has been a scandal and a shame.

When we envisage our feast of sufficiency, our great feast, I will be happy to forgo banquets in favour of a simple picnic by the lake. But we will not be a truly ecumenical celebration until everybody counts, until everyone is included: the child prostitutes and soldiers, the women whose work is sweated, the brides who are burnt, the old bent women; and they all have a name, and there is no one who is not counted.

'He has filled the hungry with good things ...'
(Luke 1, 46–55)

Of all the biblical names for Jesus, the one I love best is the Christmas one: Jesus Emmanuel, God with us. Advent for me, whatever the date, always begins when I first sing that great hymn of the church, 'O Come, o come Emmanuel'. It is based on the ancient Advent antiphons, the cries of the people beseeching God to come, to be with us. There is such longing in it, such a yearning for a different way of being, of knowing, of loving.

Emmanuel, God with us; the word made flesh, made human. It's such a huge thing, this divinity made to be one of us. There's still a tendency, perhaps a hangover from medieval ways of understanding, to think of Mary, as all women bearing children used to be thought of, merely as a container, a carrier, a surrogate giving hospitality in her womb to a self-contained potential placed there by a potent male, or male god. The truth is far more extraordinary. This Jesus, this god with us, is bone of our bone and flesh of our flesh through Mary, through the explosive communion of this woman, whose DNA he bears, and the holy spirit of God, however we understand that to have come about. I wonder sometimes, did he look like her, have her colouring, her temperament, did they say of him, 'oh, he's awful like his mammy'?

Through Mary, Jesus was one of us. But he was also God with us.

It's such a profound and moving thing, God identified so closely with humankind; it's so personal, that it can be very easy to privatise Emmanuel. God is with *me*, my possession, my personal good, my place to go when the world is giving me a hard time or I'm feeling sorry for myself. My own private spirituality, comforting, not too uncomfortably demanding, not to be talked about very much, not relevant to non-Christians; for me Jesus saves and the rest of the world carries on very much as before. In an individualistic culture, it's easy to slip into Emmanuel, God with me, and maybe people like me.

But the name is Emmanuel, God with us. In a rather revolutionary way, God with Jews and Moslems, Buddhists and Hindus, humanists and people who don't believe anything very much at all. The first chapter of John's gospel, that great poem of the word becoming flesh, takes this wider view. It takes the view that when God, in Jesus, took human nature, everything changed.

People and places, plants and animals, wood and precious stones, oil and water and bread, all of these were illuminated by his coming. The shockwaves penetrated deep beneath the surface to the existence of things – the shape of our relationships, the cast of our imaginations, the very form of our reasoning were transformed by the coming of Jesus Emmanuel. In Jesus, the pattern of reality is revealed. The whole groaning creation, not just some select groups, is part of the destiny of salvation.

But what does this mean when you bring it down to earth. Does it mean that because in Jesus, human flesh was hallowed, made holy, all humanity is made holy? I believe it. So that has implications for us far beyond our personal spiritual fulfilment. Not that our salvation is unimportant, far from it. But it is inextricably tied up with that of others, of the whole creation.

This is hard for us to engage with: easier by far to concentrate on our own souls, the little we have some control over. The anxiety and pain of anything else is acute.

But it is exactly this anxiety and pain we are called to be pregnant with. We too are part of the whole creation groaning as if in childbirth, waiting for the glory to be revealed. There is always a measure of anxiety and pain involved in pregnancy and childbirth, and for Mary, perhaps there was more than for many women, given the rather trying circumstances. And yet hers is the *great* New Testament song of liberation. She anticipates the nature of the glory, and she names it and she celebrates it. This is what glory looks like ... *He has scattered the proud with all their plans ... He has lifted up the lowly ... He has filled the hungry with good things, and sent the rich away with empty hands.* This is how it will be. Mary is the prophet of the poor, announcing the transformed social order. The spiritual realm is embedded in economic and political reality.

And the anxiety and pain of engagement with the economic and political realities of our world contain that same promise of glory, embedded deep within them, a cosmic liberation in which the hungry will be filled with good things. *'When a woman is about to give birth, she is sad because her hour of suffering has come, but when the baby is born, she forgets her suffering; because she is happy that a baby has been born into the world'* (John 16, 21). If we share the anxiety and pain, we need to remember that we also share the promise of glory, our Jubilee hope in times of change.

Where there is no Peace

(Luke 2, 8–20)

You may be surprised to hear this, but over the last few years, I've become very keen on angels. I have a friend who also likes angels and just recently she actually sent me one, which blows a trumpet and shines beautifully in the light. In case you're wondering, I should tell you that it's a stained-glass angel she made herself. And someone else who heard me preaching about angels also gave me one; she found it remaindered in the Christmas sales with a broken wing, looking forlorn, so she bought it, took it home and mended its broken wing and kept it for me till the next time she saw me, which was about a year later. This imperfect but very dear angel also keeps watch over my living-room, all the year round, not just at Christmas.

But I like at this time of year to imagine a whole bevy of angels crowding the sky and singing their hearts out, because it so happens that all the angels I've met recently, and there have been a few, have all been very good singers. But I don't want to concentrate on their singing so much as on another characteristic which angels are well-known for, and which I've also found to be true to experience, that is, – angels bring messages which change things – in fact, which change people's lives often in the most dramatic way.

The reading we heard from Luke's gospel reminds us of a wonderful message: of good news, of great joy to all the people, of glory to God and peace on earth. What could be a better message? Peace on earth.

When I thought about these words a series of pictures flashed through my mind, pictures I've met or heard from in the last few months. I want to tell you about some of them. Two weeks ago I was

14

in Northern Ireland, at the Corrymeela Community, taking part in a consultation on violence against women, and on how people in the churches can challenge this. There, I met some women from situations which are anything but peaceful.

I met Irina, a child psychologist from Minsk in Belorussia who works with survivors of the Chernobyl nuclear disaster. About 70% of the fall-out from Chernobyl fell on Belorussia, and now within this area, one in three people have been affected. Cancer of the thyroid has increased by 200%. People were forbidden to leave the area; there was little or no treatment; and most of the effects were subjected to a great cover-up. As ever, it was the children who suffered most. Can you imagine the agony of women who had to face the choice of giving their children food they knew to be contaminated, or seeing them starve? Or the mothers of the many babies subsequently born with deformities? Can you imagine the horror of the young men involved in the clear-up operation without adequate protection, who knew they were a danger to their families, or the guilt and self-loathing of the men who simply could not cope, took to drinking, left their families? Remember the violence of Chernobyl. *Remember Irina.*

And I met Françoise from the Gabon in Africa, facing the violence in France that black immigrants face all over our 'civilised' continent – the insults, the graffiti, the attacks, the fear, above all the isolation. Remember the violence of racism. *Remember Françoise.*

I met Kirsten from Sweden and Martina from Germany, concerned with issues of domestic violence. Did you know that in affluent, cultured Sweden, one woman each week is killed by her partner, or that in Germany a child is sexually abused every three minutes, and a woman is raped every four minutes? Or that here in Scotland, fifty women and their children flee their homes every day to escape domestic violence? For all of these, home is not a safe haven of love, but a place of anxiety, pain and terror. Remember the violence of abuse. *Remember Kirsten and Martina.*

And I met Neda, a Croatian woman who lives in Belgrade in

former Yugoslavia. Neda is one of the 30% of people in that tortured region who is in a mixed marriage. In her 75-year-old body, which has endured war, oppression and totalitarianism many times already, all the agony and absurdity of that war is summed up. Her parents had a mixed ethnic-group marriage. She had one. Her three sons all have such marriages. Her five grandchildren all have different ethnic identities. In her immediate family, there are eight different identities. Different, and yet all human, all bound together by marriage, love and choice. What could ethnic cleansing possibly mean for them? Every Wednesday, this elderly woman dresses in black and goes to stand with about fifty other women in the centre of Belgrade in silence. Known as the Women in Black, they do this to protest their opposition to the war, to resist being swallowed up in hatred, to be dissenters from the culture of violence. For this, they are abused, sworn at and attacked. *Remember Neda*.

Earlier on this autumn, also in Northern Ireland, I met Chrissie. Sixteen years ago, when she was seven months pregnant with their son, her 25-year-old husband was shot dead in front of his home and died in her arms. The fact that it was a case of mistaken identity seems entirely beside the point. In the practice of violence, innocent people always get hurt. *Remember Chrissie*.

And just this week in her Christmas letter, one friend had this to say: '*we have felt very close to our extended Rwandan family, as they deal with the loss of most of their close relatives – parents, brother, sister, sister-in-law, nephews, nieces and many other relatives and friends were all killed in the brutal genocide which claimed so many lives in the terrible war in Rwanda. It is difficult to comprehend, let alone understand the anguish of those left behind.*' And another, who works for an aid agency wrote of the horrors of Goma camp in Zaire: '*where the sight of traumatised kids with gaping machete wounds won't leave me …*'

Peace on earth. Goodwill to all. You could see it as a rather sick joke. You could see it as a warm blanket of false optimism, pretty words and pretty stories to wrap around us, shutting out the reality of violence, injustice, war and huge agony. Sometimes you could cry, as

Jeremiah did thousands of years ago, *'why do you cry, peace, peace, when there is no peace?' (Jeremiah 6, 14),* and be angry with God. There have been times when I have thought and felt all of these. But maybe there's a different way to understand the message of the angels, which is, after all, a message for *us*!

Perhaps it is a universal human tendency to so much want things to be clear, direct, simple, to reach an end, to be resolved. We want to wake up on Christmas morning and find that peace has broken out all over the world, that all the fighting has stopped. We want there to be a decisive action, a simple directive, a final word. To that end, we will often indulge in absurd logic. I remember talking to a friend during the Gulf War, in the final days before the bombing deadline ran out. She was opposed to the war, but she said, 'I wish now they'd just get on with the bombing, so that the war can be over.' And I know I live with the hope, somewhere at the back of my mind, that someday there will be a dramatic gesture, a prophetic outpouring, a great conversion, a miracle, that will cut through the tedium and bring peace.

But we don't get that. What we get is a baby born into a dangerous and impoverished world. Not a miracle, just a baby. One, moreover, who had to flee as a refugee from the swords of war, whose life and teaching led him into conflict, and who ended up dying violently and ignominiously. Peace didn't break out the day he was born either!

When I look at Jesus, it doesn't seem to me that his way of true peace was any different, or easier, or any more spectacular, than ours is today. It was the way of Irina, who goes on with the children of Chernobyl, and says, 'People work for each other, support each other, and know that their salvation and hope comes in involvement.' It is the way of Françoise and Kirsten and Martina, continuing to stand against racism and domestic violence, the way of Neda standing in a Belgrade square dressed in black for the third war in her lifetime. It is the way of Chrissie, painfully rebuilding her life, finding new meaning in working with people with learning difficulties and deeply committed to the peace process in Northern Ireland. It is the way of my friend's Rwandan family, who insist that the only way forward is reconciliation. It is the way of people who hold on to justice and let go of revenge, who hold on to peace and let go of violence, who hold on to love and let go of hate. It is the way of people who let go of death and hold on to new life.

If these people, who have suffered and lost so much, have confronted the worst horrors of violence, can go on in peace, and not just stoically but with humour and love and hope, this to me is an angelic message indeed. And when, this Christmas, I think I hear the angels singing, they will have faces and names, of women and men who follow Jesus in making the word flesh, in *living* peace on earth and goodwill to all, in glorifying God by their conviction that God coming in Jesus made all of life holy and to be cherished.

I think this message of peace is not just one that is lived in Rwanda and Bosnia and Minsk and Belfast. It's for all the warring situations in our own lives – all our smaller but no less real war zones, in our hearts and homes, in our families and communities, in our country. Because I know that so many of *you* are living peace against the violence of homelessness, loneliness, fear and poverty right here in this city, I will also see your faces among the angels this Christmas.

In this year of his centenary, I feel I can do no better than finish with some words from Robert Louis Stevenson's Christmas Sermon, and pray that we may find the blessing of living peace this Christmas.

> *But the task before us, which is to co-endure with our existence, is rather one of microscopic fineness, and the heroism required is that of patience. There is no cutting of the Gordian knots of life; each must be smilingly unravelled … and the knot that we cut by some fine heady quarrel-scene in private life, or, in public affairs, by some denunciatory act against what we are pleased to call our neighbour's vices, might yet have been unwoven by the hand of sympathy.*

Carrying
our own Crosses

(Jeremiah 18, 1–11, Luke 14, 25–33)

*Jesus said to them, 'whoever does not carry his own cross and
come after me cannot be my disciple.'*

A couple of days ago, I read a rather unedifying report in the
newspaper of what passes for public spectacle in the tragic land
of Afghanistan. The report describes the events that take place on
Fridays in the national sports stadium – not, alas, football or athletics,
but the rather more gruesome spectator sport of hangings, floggings
and amputations. The crowd apparently numbers around 3000 people,
and children sell cola and popcorn.

Before judging such a people, and such a country, too harshly,
however, it is also worth noting that this is a country ruled by a
fanatical and extremist regime, where the Taliban militias have banned
almost every kind of entertainment; television, cinema, video, theatre,
music and dancing and the drinking of alcohol are all forbidden, and
the penalties for flouting the ban are severe, and could indeed include
ending up as one of those being flogged or having one's limbs cut off.
Furthermore, it is a country where women, who have borne the brunt
of the fanaticism, are forbidden to work, to be educated or to be seen
outside the home – a problem not least for the thousands of war
widows who are the sole support of their families.

In such an arid cultural climate, it is not hard to see how
anything happening at all, even something as macabre as a public
execution, would attract a crowd, especially if you want to keep on the

right side of the authorities staging the event. Palestine in the time of Christ had none of the kinds of entertainment that we take for granted, and though there is no evidence that music and dancing were also banned, still it was a society which was unchanging and routine enough in everyday life for anything out of the ordinary to draw a crowd. Public executions were a feature of life then too, and there is no reason to suppose that the crowd which gathered to watch Jesus being crucified was much different from those cheering in the national stadium in Kabul.

Even in this country, you can gather a crowd quite quickly on Sauchiehall Street, though we hope mostly for the more innocent pleasures of listening to a fast-tongued street trader or watching a piece of outdoor theatre. Jesus was enough of an attraction to draw big crowds wherever he went, and there is much evidence in the gospels to suggest that he did not always welcome the attention. Like today's beleaguered celebrities, he tried various strategies to retain some privacy and solitude, some peace and quiet out of the public glare: he tried going up mountains, into friends' houses; he even went as far as thinking he could get away in a boat on the lake. You can just see the kinds of headlines the tabloids might have about him today above the paparazzi photographs of a smudged figure in the middle of the Sea of Galilee: 'local man escapes crowds; neighbours talk of the good boy they used to know who turned vagrant'. 'I blame the company he keeps, says one.'

But in today's passage from Luke's gospel, we see him doing something quite different. The usual large crowds of people were accompanying him, and we can imagine the noise, the chat, the children with the Palestinian equivalent of cola and popcorn, and Jesus in the middle, getting somewhat frustrated. This was a point in his three-year ministry when the crowd was still with him: they liked what he was saying; they liked the fact that he healed people; they liked it that he had time for the ordinary people. Things had not yet begun to get really dangerous. You can see how Jesus might think: 'they haven't got a clue; they think this is a picnic', and stopping, might turn round and challenge them to listen to what it really meant to follow him.

He didn't mince his words, did he? You can just hear him, looking for the words that could properly convey the seriousness of what following him meant. 'You can't be my disciple unless you love me more than you love your father and mother, more than your spouse and your children, more than your brothers and sisters, more even than you love your own life.' These words would carry great weight in a culture in which family was everything. Even in our more individualistic society, they are hard words to hear.

And then, to add emphasis, 'Unless you carry your own cross and come after me, you can't be my disciple!' There is a profoundly shocking element in these words. We hear them as religious words, they are familiar to us in the context of commitment; but we rarely are in the position where we hear them literally. But to the crowd following Jesus, their meaning was much more raw. They were accustomed to the public executions that were all too familiar in a country under foreign occupation, and one of the features of these public executions was that those being killed first had to carry their own crosses, their own death weapons, to the place of execution. Jesus saying that was exactly parallel to the situation of the Jews killed in Germany, the Moslems killed in Bosnia, who first had to dig their own graves, knowing they would then be shot and pushed into them. Jesus was really saying, if you want to follow me, you have to first dig your own grave, you have to carry the possibility of your death for my sake with you.

Most of us don't think about our faith in that way. We live in a democracy, in peaceful times; we are not persecuted for our faith or our political beliefs, or (most of us) for our race or gender or sexual orientation. We don't have to think about the ultimate cost of discipleship as a daily reality. And few of us have the rigour, for example, of the Catholic religious order who used to sleep every night in their shrouds, as a reminder that their lives were already dead, and buried with Christ in God; nor of John Wesley, who used to say that a Christian should be ready to preach, pray or die at any moment.

This famous passage from Luke's gospel is subtitled in the Good News Bible as *The Cost of Discipleship*, and the earlier part of the chapter is all about the kinds of attachments which prevent people from living in God's way. There was the story of the man Jesus healed on the Sabbath. There was the story of the wedding feast at which those who sat in the lowest places were taken to the seats of honour and those who took the best places were humbled. And there was the story of the great feast where all those invited made excuses of one kind or another, and their places were given to the poor, the lame and the people in the streets and alleys.

All of these were ways in which Jesus was trying to show the crowds, and prepare his disciples, for the demands of true discipleship, and to evoke the kind of commitment that the love of God required. These demands and commitments made everything else secondary; and it's worth reflecting that they are not any less demanding now than they were then. By and large, they are extremely countercultural, whatever one's culture. Jesus said:

- If a person is in need, that need takes precedence, is more important, than religious laws.
- The needs of the poor are a greater priority than your own social life.
- Neither work nor financial interest nor family relationships, not even being newly-wed, are to come between us and the call of God.

There is possibly no passage in the Bible which spells out so starkly the wholehearted love of God which is necessary to follow Jesus. Of course, this is not to say that any of these things are particularly wrong or bad in themselves. Clearly that is not the case. Most often, it is in loving attentiveness to these things that our discipleship is expressed.

But he is saying that if any of these things – work, family, economics, personal life, the law of church or state, even our own survival – becomes more important, more binding than the love of God, then we fall into idolatry, and move further from the kingdom. There may be times when we have to make choices.

Though the crowds, and even the disciples, had not fully realised the implication of Jesus's challenge to the status quo, Jesus himself understood that the way ahead was not smooth and untroubled. I suppose, like all people in positions of leadership, he would have liked to have a dream team, perfect followers, people who could cope with all that the future would bring – people who were, say, reliable, enthusiastic, informed, resourceful and psychologically well-balanced. As it was, he had a bunch of uneducated fishermen, peasant farmers, social misfits and outcasts, and at least one potentially dangerous political extremist. That's to say, he had the people who showed up, human beings with all their strengths and weaknesses, all their flaws and their gifts. These were the ones he had walked the highways and byways of Palestine for three years with, the ones he had tried so hard to explain his faith, his ministry, his relationship to God with; and for much of the time, they had failed to understand. But they were still there, flaws and all, and by this time, that was what counted.

And now, once again, Jesus tried to prepare them for what lay ahead. He uses the example of planning two different kinds of tasks: a building and a military campaign. For both of these to succeed, they need to be properly thought out, costed in terms of resources, personnel, equipment. Anyone can see that. In the first example, Jesus is asking, can you afford to pay this cost? In the second, he is asking, can you afford *not* to pay it? But most of all, he wants to be plain and truthful with them about what they have let themselves in for.

These are vivid and striking examples of what it means to take seriously the cost of discipleship. And yet even they are limited in their scope. If you plan a building, and you have the necessary resources, you have a pretty good chance of seeing it completed according to your plan. If you embark on a military campaign and you have the superior force and arms, then mostly, though not always, you can be confident of winning. With both of them, there is a reasonable chance of predicting the outcome. But to follow Jesus was, and is, not so predictable. However we prepare, however much we think we have our plans worked out, we do not know the mind of God, nor can we control the circumstances in which our discipleship will be tested.

Indeed, perhaps loving God for us is less like being an architect or a general, and more like the experience that Jeremiah described in this morning's other reading. Perhaps we are more like clay in the potter's hands, continually being reworked, being remoulded until our imperfections are smoothed away. This was the experience of the disciples, both before and after the death of Jesus, finding themselves in situations and facing challenges that nothing in their experience could have prepared them for, and yet finding that God took their imperfections and made them into the people who were needed. It was the experience of the German Lutheran pastor Dietrich Bonhoeffer, who in 1937 wrote a book called *The Cost of Discipleship*, and in 1945 found himself paying that cost when he was executed for his part in the plot to assassinate Hitler.

One of the most extraordinary and humbling experiences of attending the last Lambeth Conference was to meet and hear the stories of men and women who, in very different circumstances in different parts of the world, must reckon with the high cost of discipleship: bishops in the Sudan, for example, divided north and south, whose people are both dying of hunger and racked by war; bishops in Rwanda who had lost every member of their families in the genocide of 1994; the bishop from Myanmar, Burma, who had just been released from eleven months under house arrest; the bishop of Iran, whose predecessor was murdered and who lives in constant danger. The stories are legion, and they left me in no doubt both of the cost of discipleship, but even more of the love and joy that sustains these people through the most appalling trials.

Faced with such models of courage and faith, I could only give thanks, and feel a bit ashamed by my own smallness of discipleship. And yet we too, Christians in this country, have our own tasks of faithfulness given to us by God, and we need not be ashamed of them; for they are what the Lord requires of us here: to support our brothers and sisters across the world in our prayers and practical service; to be witnesses in our own situations and community to the unconditional love of God; to point in our lives to the self-offering of Jesus for our healing. We may do this in very small, undramatic ways in our life as a church with open doors, in relationship with the many people who come through them, and in our own personal lives and work. In all of this, the God who shapes and remakes our lives as the potter shapes the clay is making us what we need to be. The cost for us is in our willingness to let ourselves be clay, to trust to the hands of God, and to let God be God in our lives. In this, I think we need not be afraid. This is the God who, as Psalm 139 reminds us, protects us with power and knows us beyond our understanding.

Stand Firm

(Isaiah 65, 17–25, Luke 21, 5–19)

Stand firm and you will save yourselves
(Luke 21, 19)

It would have been quite easy in these past few months to look around the world and the times we live in and see in them the troubles and persecutions Jesus described in today's lectionary reading from the New Testament. Countries are fighting each other in the Balkans, in Central Africa and in dozens of low-level conflicts all over the world. There have been terrible floods in Bangladesh, hurricanes sweeping Central America and the Caribbean, earthquakes in China, famines in the wake of all of these, diseases that were thought to have been eradicated, such as smallpox and tuberculosis, are returning on the backs of poverty and malnutrition. And one can readily imagine that for a Honduran, Hurricane Mitch fits the description of a strange and terrifying thing coming from the sky; or indeed that ordinary Iraqis even now are waiting with fear and trepidation for other strange and terrifying things coming from the sky.

It is a well-established fact that the end of centuries have a strange effect on the collective psyche, that in some ways a kind of madness breaks out, and that this is particularly evident in the mushrooming of sects and cults of many kinds, especially those who anticipate the end of the world. They are to be found in every religion, and in those of extremely obscure beliefs. At the end of the first millennium since the time of Christ this tendency was multiplied many times, and there are signs that this is also the case at the end of this millennium. There are plenty of people who are quite convinced that the so-called 'millennium bug', whereby computers which are not programmed to adapt to the numerical change from 1999 to 2000 are liable to crash and throw the systems they run into chaos, is a manifestation of the end times.

On the other hand, you don't need a somewhat random date for people to have had this feeling. Over the last week, like many of you perhaps, I watched a number of documentaries and read a number of articles about the First World War, which ended eighty years ago this week. Their descriptions of the indescribable hell of the trenches, of men living for months and sometimes years in underground holes up to their knees in vermin and putrid human waste and dismembered body parts, of rampant disease and relentless bombardment, of the millions upon millions of young men, a whole generation of European youth, who dutifully lined up and mowed each other down defy the imagination. Many then thought they were living in the end times – all the biblical signs were there.

And the signs were there too in 17th-century Europe, during the Thirty Years War, interminable religious conflicts that raged back and forth across Europe, rendering much of it a blackened charnel house in which millions, not only soldiers, were butchered, starved, or frozen to death, or perished in one of the periodic outbreaks of the Black Death. Oh, and almost a million women were burned as witches. There were many then who thought they were living in the end times.

Historians tell us that one of the main factors which brought about the Enlightenment, the Age of Reason in the 18th century, which saw the value of freedom of conscience, religious tolerance and the move towards democracy, was that Europe was simply exhausted, nauseated to the point of death by a century of religious wars and the destruction of habitats, and something like common sense finally prevailed. The value and importance of simply being human, of the right to life, broke through the culture of death and the competing ideologies. To be human, and to be able to live in peace and make a living, finally came to seem more important than being Catholic or Protestant, than being French or Austrian, than being any particular tribe or group.

After the Armistice too, there was a sense not just of an ending but of a beginning. Lloyd George talked about the war to end all wars, and the soldiers came wearily home from the front to a society which had changed for ever, one in which the old privileges of class and status would never again hold quite the same power, one which they hoped would become 'a land fit for heroes'. For the returning heroes, the aspirations were much the same as they were for the worn-out civilians of Europe in the 17th century: peace, a place to live, the means to support their families; these were not huge demands, just the hopes of being human. It was not so long before such hopes were cruelly dashed; the high spirits of the 1920s gave way to the stock market crashes of Wall Street and the great Depression, which in turn gave way to the rise of fascism and the Second World War.

The Old Testament lectionary reading this morning paints an almost diametrically opposed picture to that of Luke's gospel. Here is the prophet writing around the 5th century BC, at a time after the return from the long Babylonian exile. Neighbouring countries had been harrying a small defenceless country, economic conditions were dire, and though the temple had been rebuilt, Jerusalem was still in ruins. The people were despondent. This too was a country facing the task of reconstruction, daunted by the enormity of the task and, under these huge constraints and problems, faltering in its faith. So the prophet, seeking to revive faith and encourage those growing faint of heart, drew this glowing picture of God's new creation, a picture which has encouraged and inspired countless generations ever since.

Here is the promise of a new heaven and a new earth, and it resonates across the centuries, for, in truth, the hope it holds out is very little different from the hope of the 17th century, or of Europe after the Great War, or indeed of men and women today, whether in Honduras or Kosovo or the Congo or even Iraq. In this new heaven and earth, the memories of past suffering will no longer haunt the mind. Babies will no longer die in infancy; adults will live out their lifespan. No one will be homeless; no one will plant vineyards and have others take the fruits. And above all, there will be peace: even nature will be peaceful; the very snakes will not be dangerous. Here, there will be nothing dangerous or evil. There will be no more weeping, only joy. It is the hope of being human.

It's a remarkably simple and gentle vision, this. A home, good health, a way to make a living and enjoy modest fruits, the wellbeing of one's loved ones, harmony with the natural world and peace. It seems so simple, so unremarkable, that it becomes almost intolerable, almost incredible that it should be such an unattainable vision in a world so full of riches. Of course, there are plenty of us in the world who enjoy at least most of these things. We are the lucky ones. But even for us, we do not live untouched by the rest of the world. We inhabit the same planet. In the last 25 years, humankind has destroyed 30%, *30%*, almost a third of the world's natural resources. The responsibility for this falls very heavily on the wealthy countries of the West. A hundred years from now, our great-grandchildren may live in a very different world from us, where wars may be fought over water and other natural resources. They will inherit our legacy. There is no guarantee that they will inherit the earth.

In the Lucan passage, Jesus, like the prophets before him, warned the disciples against thinking they could predict when the end times would come. The knowledge of that would be God's alone; even the Son of Man did not know the hour. And he warned them further of even harder times to come. Like the prophets, Jesus foresaw no rose-strewn path for the people of God. But in the midst even of disaster, persecution and chaos, his followers were neither to panic and flee, nor to become fanatical and obsessed. Rather, they were to understand such circumstances to be a chance for them to proclaim the good news, what the book of Isaiah calls the good news of deliverance. So, even in the face of hatred, betrayal and the threat of death, they were to stand firm and speak the words that Jesus would give them.

One of the threads that links the passage from Isaiah and the passage from Luke is the temple in Jerusalem. The first speaks in a time when the temple had just been rebuilt, the first part of reconstruction after the war. Jesus speaks of the tearing down of the temple, and the destruction that is to come. These two themes are like a point and counterpoint in music, like thesis and antithesis, like negative and positive, attraction and repulsion, two opposite forces contending with one another throughout history. Always there is this pull towards destruction, and beside and before and beyond it, the pull towards rebuilding, restoration, towards the new creation. For the Jews, the temple was the symbol of the new creation, built on Zion's sacred hill. And indeed, forty years after Jesus, the temple was once again destroyed, and it has been destroyed and rebuilt since then.

But there is a strange thing about Jesus and the temple. You will remember that at the very moment of his death on the cross, the curtain hanging in the temple was torn from top to bottom. That curtain was the one which guarded the inmost sanctum of the temple, the Holy of Holies, in which the Ark of the Covenant was kept. So holy was it that only the High Priest could enter, and he only once a year. It was the sacred place of access to God. Christians understand the tearing of the curtain to mean that no longer was God found in a place, directly accessible only to the few and mediated through them. Now God had come close to humankind, closer than breathing, because God had become human in Jesus. No longer was God exclusive. Now life in God was possible for everyone human, because God had hallowed humanity in the incarnation, death and resurrection of Jesus.

When Jesus called his disciples to stand firm and tell the good news, he was asking them to bear witness to the new creation, the new heaven and earth, in the midst of death and destruction. No matter what was going on around them, they were to bear witness to the promise of *new life*. Because of that promise, they need not be afraid. Not a single hair of their heads would be lost. No witness to new life is ever lost. They were to bear witness to the possibility of being fully human.

Always in human societies there has been the destructive urge to limit who is human, to compare and exclude. At different times and in different places, black lives have been considered less fully human than white lives, female lives less than male, Protestant lives less than Catholic, and vice versa, Moslem lives less than Christian, Jewish lives less than Aryan, Palestinian lives less than Israeli, homosexual lives less than heterosexual. And always, including today, the lives of poor, strange or marginalised people have been considered less fully human, less precious, more expendable than the lives of rich people. Whatever we may say to the contrary, as long as we continue to extort blood money from the poorest countries in interest for debts whose capital has long since been repaid, we are practising the belief that the lives of poor people are more expendable, less fully human than the lives of rich people. As long as we continue to degrade the environment to satisfy the appetites of energy-extravagant Westerners, this is what we are practising.

In his parables and teachings, Jesus reached out again and again to the people whom the world excluded or counted as valueless, and included them in the human community: women, foreigners, prostitutes, thieves and publicans, the sick, the mentally deranged, the poorest of the poor. He held them up as being closer to the kingdom than the righteous and the respectable. To stand firm for the good news of the kingdom is to stand for a just and inclusive community, for living in order that others may live and enjoy the sufficient life of the new creation, and most of all to stand for the inexhaustible love and mercy of God for all human sinners.

George MacLeod, the Founder of the Iona Community, wrote:

> *Our congregations miss the zest of the early Christian church because we have forgotten the glorious emancipation of our true humanity that was the Incarnation. Jesus the carpenter, the friend of shepherds and fishermen, showed us God by being human – and in three days set at naught the complex temple that was forty years in building. He made risen humanity his temple. We must be human.*

Sharing
our Bread

(1 Corinthians 11, 23–26)

For I received from the Lord the teaching that I passed on to you:
that the Lord Jesus, on the night he was betrayed, took a piece of bread, gave
thanks to God, broke it, and said 'This is my body, which is for you.
Do this in memory of me.' (1 Cor. 11, 23–24)

'The great community problem of our modern world is how to share bread.'

These words were said by George MacLeod, the Founder of the Iona Community, several decades ago. They are no less true now than they were then. More so, for we know that the gap between the rich of the earth, among whom we must count ourselves, and the earth's poor, after 30 post-war years of narrowing, has been followed by 20 years in which it has got wider – so wide that there has never been a time in human history when it was so great, or affected so many people. Truly, Lazarus is far away.

I thought about these words a couple of days ago, when I was reading the morning paper, as one does, turning over the pages that so graphically describe the troubles and persecutions, the awful horror, flicking through, as one does, the wars and rumours of wars, the famines and earthquakes, filing away the information in my very well-informed mind over my toast. Then, just as I was thinking it was time to get a move on, I was grabbed by the scruff of the neck and slammed up against the wall by the Lord God Almighty, as one is.

At the bottom of the page, I read a story of a child, a small 12-

year-old Kenyan boy, who had set out to be an illegal immigrant into Britain – or maybe into somewhere else, who knows if he knew where he was bound – by climbing high up under a jet plane and into the tiny space behind the wheel carriage. But when the wheels retracted, they retracted back into his body, and he was crushed to death, suffering terrible injuries. He had no identification, no name, but it is thought that he was probably one of 40,000 street children who live in Nairobi. I read the story, and I found myself weeping uncontrollably for an African child. I don't know why it was his story, and not the one about the Romanian orphans with AIDS, or the Albanian children being hosed on a southern beach, or the 11-year-old Thai child prostitute. It just was. As I said, for me it was a word from the Lord, reminding me that the great community problem of our modern world is how to share bread.

I remembered these words again when I thought about the Last Supper, about Jesus sharing bread with his disciples. Is this how we are to share bread, loving our friends to the end, tender, intimate, serving one another? My life has been based on this conviction. But I found myself caught on the lethal point of contradiction between the gospel story and the newspaper one. The reality of our world is that we, having bread, decide who will get to eat it. And the poor are still hungry.

Bread, of course, as well as being real, also stands as a symbol for other things – for homes, clothes, healthcare, work, hope, justice – all the things that Jesus was always banging on about, the necessities of life, the wherewithal to sustain life. Water, too. Ironically, in the same newspaper, I also read about the land that is being parched of water so that jaded Western palates can have mangetout peas in season and out of it. Kenyan land!

We go to great lengths, do we not, to protect our right to control who will get bread. We protect our interests, our shares, our boundaries, our freedom in the markets of the globe at every level. And mostly, it's hard to see that the church does anything more than mirror the world. We, having bread, decide who we will permit to share it – and not only to share it, but to break it and distribute it, though we are not always so interested in those who make it or bake it.

I am a mother, and every day my children sit down at the table and I feed them. Before I serve them, before I permit them to eat, I don't ask them if they've been good, or tell them they must confess all their wrongdoing before they get anything. I don't ask them whether they love me, and make it a condition of their eating. I even feed their friends, and I know they don't love me. I feed them because they're hungry, and because I love *them*. And so do you! Oh, I know you could say I'm being simplistic, and perhaps I am, but on this night, of all nights, I have to face up to the challenge behind the evasions and the sophistications. We confess a God who is father of us all, a motherly God who feeds us for no other reason than that we are hungry, a God who spoke in a man who said, 'I was hungry and you fed me.' Sometimes I think that if Jesus had known what would be done to and with bread in his name, he would have wept! Well, of course, he did. We taint and corrupt everything. *Lamb of God, you take away the sin of the world. Have mercy upon us.*

'I hate your religious festivals; stop your noisy songs; instead, let justice roll like a river, and righteousness like a stream that never runs dry' (Amos 5, 21–24). So spoke the prophet, and, indeed, if we get so caught up in the perfection of our Holy Week remembrance, or the beauty of our ceremonies and prayers, or our own nourishment, that we forget that people are still hungry and we are embodied with them in Christ's body, then we rather miss the point of Jesus the bread of life. The bread was broken to be shared.

For me, the only way I can come to communion tonight is knowing my own emptiness, my own failures in sharing, my complicity with the world order into which I was born, my original sin. Conversion, turning away from that order to God's economy of sharing, is hard. I am hungry to change, and that hunger I cannot satisfy myself. So I will stretch out my hand, and I will be fed; not because I am good or deserving, but because I am loved, and it is in the nature of God to feed hungry children. By grace alone are we fed. And when I hear the words, 'this is my body', I will remember the total identification of Jesus with all flesh, and I will see his body broken in a small boy dying beneath the wings of a plane. God give us grace to share our bread.

Speak to Make
a New World Possible

(John 20, 19–31)

… but Jesus came and stood among them and said, 'Peace be with you.'
Then he said to Thomas, 'Put your finger here and look at my hands; then
stretch out your hand and put it in my side …' (John 20, 26–7)

The resurrection story of Thomas the doubter never fails to surprise me, no matter how many times I hear it. It's not the disciples who surprise me, huddled and afraid behind locked doors. That's what people do after violent deaths; they hide, unless even their hiding place is taken away from them, and who can blame them? Traumatised, terrorised and bereft, of course they were hiding. It does seem a little strange, to be sure, that when Jesus suddenly appears, giving them the conventional, customary greeting 'Peace be with you', they react with delight, not, as one might expect, with confusion, with fear, with horror, even. It all seems remarkably matter of fact.

It says a great deal about their relationship with him that they didn't react in the way you or I might if our recently dead friend suddenly materialised through a closed door. It suggests a very high level of trust that whatever he did: they believed in his commitment to their wellbeing. They knew he would do nothing to hurt them. But it also reminds us that for three years they had followed him, travelled with him and loved him, while mostly not having a clue what was going on. Their relationship with him and his work was so characterised by misunderstanding, perplexity and just plain getting it wrong that you almost get a sense of 'oh … this is different … but whatever it is, I like it!'

Nor am I surprised by Thomas's hesitation, though I know there's a pious tradition that one is supposed to be shocked by his lack of faith. Presumably with serious concerns for the sanity of his friends, his response seems the most natural thing in the world, responsible even. He's a prototype for all the judges who've ever said, 'let me see the evidence', for all the parents who've ever said 'give me proof you've been where you say', for every lover who ever sang, 'don't talk of stars, shining above, if you're in love, show me'. There's no evidence to suppose Jesus himself wouldn't have been pretty sympathetic to Thomas; doubt played a part in his makeup too, and he was fond of singing some of the most agonised of the Psalms.

Actually, I like Thomas a lot; for his resolute common sense and his steadfast refusal to conform his questioning mind to the general rejoicing, for having the courage to hang on to his truth, for letting doubt into the canon. But most of all, I like him because he's one of the people in the Bible who recognises the importance of bodies. Perhaps it's because he was a twin. I imagine a tiny Thomas in the womb, entwined with another tiny body from his earliest sense memory, suckling at one breast while a sibling suckled at the other, always close to the sight and smell and touch of another's flesh.

Be that as it may, without Thomas, we would not know that thing which always surprises me, for it is not mentioned in any of the other gospels – that the risen Jesus was still wounded, that his resurrection body still bore the marks of the crucifixion. How extraordinary that is. How much we let it slide by us in the church. You would think that a resurrection body would be perfect, shining, unmarked. So much of the great religious art of the world shows the risen Christ in that way. Why shouldn't they, because that's the way Paul described it in 1st Corinthians. He said, '*This is how it will be when the dead are raised to life. When the body is buried, it is mortal, when raised it will be immortal. When buried, it is ugly and weak*' *(1 Corinthians 15, 42–43)*. Well, after the ordeal of the cross, the whipping, the falling, the nailing, the heat and the thirst, the dying, the body of Jesus would be ugly and weak. But says Paul, '*When raised it will be beautiful and strong.*' But here is a body, shown to Thomas and the other disciples, that still has scars on its hands, and a great gaping wound in its side. And, perhaps, presumably, still has callouses on its feet from so much walking, dry patches on its skin from the heat, even the odd grey hair.

I need to know that God is real, I need to know that Christ can feel … Thomas draws our attention to the body of Christ. There is a reality here that is quite disconcerting. It reiterates the picture in Matthew 28 of Jesus meeting the women in the garden, where, we are told, they take hold of his feet, and that in Luke 24, where Jesus invites his disciples to feel his hands and feet, for, he says, I have flesh and bones, unlike a ghost. The risen Jesus is substantial, material, not etherealised, spiritualised. He retains the integrity of body and soul; flesh and spirit are still one in him. In life, in death, in life beyond death, he is undivided. The resurrection is an absolutely clear message that bodies matter, that the miracle and the mystery of the incarnation, the embodiment of Jesus Christ the word made flesh is neither accidental nor incidental. It is the whole point. We know and are known in the body, we are personal only in the body, and it is as whole persons that we live and fall and die and are raised to new life.

But why, in the resurrection, still the wounds? Why not the beautiful, strong, unmarked body of Paul's vision? God knows, the attraction of the perfect body, especially as ours ages and lets us down here and there, is intense – perhaps for Paul too; he doesn't always seem very comfortable in his. Oh, but we are also our wounds.

> *I'm not a symbol*
> *I'm not a statistic*
> *I'm not the inches in somebody's column.*
> *I'm not admirable, but*
> *I'm not pitiable either.*
> *I'm simply human.*

If you turned me inside out,
you'd find fury, fear, regret and sorrow
struggling with the love and longing,
hope and wonder,
and all my neediness.

Please take these things seriously.
Don't pietise or glamorise or trivialise or sermonise.
They are the marks of my life,
gift and loss,
wound and offence.
Please respect them.
I am at odds with all that requires me to be a symbol.
I insist on being real. (Kathy Galloway)

The marks of our lives are an integral part of who we really are, as they are of Jesus. And it is in the reality of our lives that we are most personal, most relational, most loved and precious. It is that reality that reminds us that the masses huddled in misery and squalor in refugee camps across the world are not just masses, they are persons, and that the driven and fanatical soldiers of the Taliban are persons, and that the transvestites of Rio de Janeiro are persons, and that it was for persons that Christ lived and Christ died and Christ was raised. It is in our bodies, in the giftedness of them, but also in their wounds that we remember who we are. Rowan Williams writes: *Memory is the self, because it is my presence to myself, the way in which I constitute myself and understand myself as a subject with a continuous history of experience.*

But memory is first of all bodily. The smallest cell remembers a sound, words collect physical and emotional responses, hold them in the body. It is the body which remembers first; memory is what brings to mind that which is already in the body. We feel the sense memory in the body, and then we feel the emotional response that collected it in the first place: the curiosity, the delight, the wonder, or the fear, the sorrow, the anger. How could the risen body of Christ be anything other than marked with his wounds? In Christ's crucified body is named all the violence of the world. We have to remember; for if we do not remember the wounds, we will not remember the love that was greater than the violence.

I have a friend who works for an international aid agency. A couple of years ago, he visited the huge Rwandan refugee camp in the Congolese town of Goma. In his Christmas letter that year he wrote: '... but I cannot forget the great gaping machete wounds in the sides of the children ...' I cannot now think of the crucified Christ without seeing that image also, never. Christ's wounds are the wounds of the children of Goma, and Pristina and Baghdad and Omagh. But it is such a despairing image; it is so full of dread. To recall that alone is to look into hell, an eternity of Good Fridays. So the central act of the Christian community is a remembering not just of the wounded Christ, but of the wounded and risen Christ, living in the body to sustain his people.

> In the body broken and the blood poured out
> We restore to memory and hope
> The broken and unremembered victims of tyranny and sin
> (Janet Morley)

The whole Christian church is constituted on memory; it is a great litany running through the testaments from the beginning to the end: In the beginning was the Word ... remember you were a slave ... and the Word was with God ... remember who you once were ... and the Word was with God ... once you were no people ... and the Word was God ... these have been written in order that you may believe and have life ... and Thomas answered him, 'my Lord and my God'.

But it is a remembering, a coming back to the body that is not just wounded but risen. It is not memory alone that gives new life. Memory only traps us in an endless cycle of blame and guilt and pain.

Only hope can set us free. And hope comes as the word made flesh once again, here and now, *in the present*, to Mary, to Peter, to Thomas. It is the life beyond death; it is the new relationship. There is a wonderful poem by Janet Morley.

> *The bodies of grownups*
> *come with stretchmarks and scars,*
> *faces that have been lived in,*
> *relaxed breasts and bellies,*
> *backs that give trouble*
> *and well-worn feet:*
> *flesh that is particular*
> *and obviously mortal.*
> *They also come*
> *with bruises on their heart,*
> *wounds they can't forget,*
> *and each of them*
> *a company of lovers in their soul*
> *who will not return*
> *and cannot be erased.*
> *And yet I think there is a flood of beauty*
> *beyond the smoothness of youth;*
> *and my heart aches for that grace of longing*
> *that flows through bodies*
> *no longer straining to be innocent,*
> *but yearning for redemption.*

The body of Christ which Thomas feared yet longed to embrace, in all its woundedness, is our continuity with the past, with our experience, with our identity. It is familiar, all that we have and all that we are. Without the wounds, there is no consciousness of resurrection. But it is a risen body, and it is strange beyond imagining, something quite new. It is a body which speaks more loudly than words of a redemption which is born not of innocence but of sheer grace. It is a redemption which is characterised by that repeated blessing, *Peace be with you, peace be with you*. It is the life lived out of freedom and not out of the fear that is the legacy of memory alone.

And as with the body personal, so with the body corporate. Jesus breathes the divine spirit, his abiding presence, into the community of his followers and incarnates in them the responsibility of that forgiveness that he lived to the full. It is a vivid reminder of and continuity with their last supper together; it is the promise of indwelling made good.

I believe I am part of a body. But it is not just any body. It is a resurrection body. As part of that body, we carry wounds and scars, and some of them are very ugly. We carry, all of us, the torturer's wounds as well as the victims. Bearing the marks is part of that belonging. But we also have to affirm and celebrate and nurture the communal joys, the life that is given back to us through the body. We share the wounds – but we also share the life. When we minister the word made flesh to each other, we are inviting each other to embrace what is hopeful and new and strange and as intimate as indwelling. The church is often not good at this. We are experts at reminding people of the wounds, the marks. Crucifixion is not strange. It's the most wearily predictable thing in the world. You can see it on TV every night. Let us rather, in the words of Dom Helder Camara, *'honour the Word eternal, and speak to make a new world possible'*. Let us speak of acceptance and healing. Let us speak of justice and love. Let us affirm the resurrection of the wounded body of Christ.

The Good News of Deliverance

(Isaiah 61, 1–3, John 21, 1–9)

The sovereign Lord has filled me with his Spirit. (Isaiah 61, 1)
The disciple whom Jesus loved said to Peter, 'It is the Lord.' (John 21, 7)

On discovering in the lectionary what the gospel reading for today is, there's an almost irresistible temptation to be gently humorous about Peter jumping in at the deep end, and about his propensity for going fishing in the nude. This Peter will be glad to hear that it's a temptation I am going to resist. Nor, though it is the beginning of a new ministry, do I propose to draw any analogies between fish and men; once, on a religious television programme, I was asked if I had caught many men in my ministry, and replied without stopping to think *'not as many as I'd like!'* Besides, that is the kind of analogy that might have had more resonance in 1898, rather than 1998, when churches were packing them in like fish tumbled out from an overfull net. The Lord seems to have another purpose for our discipleship in these millennial times, at least in Scotland.

Rather I want to turn first to these great words from Isaiah 61, which were part of the Old Testament lectionary this morning.

The Sovereign Lord has filled me with his spirit.
He has chosen me and sent me
To bring good news to the poor,
To heal the broken-hearted,

to announce release to captives
and freedom to those in prison.
He has sent me to proclaim
That the time has come
When the Lord will save his people.

You will remember that it is these words that Jesus chose to read in the synagogue in Nazareth, and to lay claim to as his own, as a way of announcing the task and the journey he was setting out on. It was a mighty statement of purpose which has come to be known as the Lucan Manifesto (Luke 4, 16–30) and profoundly significant to his listeners in his home town, those people who had known him all his life as simply 'Joseph's son'. Because, of course, it was a claim to Messiahship, to being the long-expected one, the saviour of Israel. A quite shattering claim for a home-town boy, a carpenter's son. And you will remember too that they didn't like it at all, thought it so arrogant, so uncomfortable that they turned into a lynch mob, and were quite ready to throw him off a cliff.

But let's look back at these great words, this good news of deliverance. Where did they come from in the first place? To whom were they spoken originally? The prophecies contained in the book of Isaiah were written in the latter half of the 8th century BC. These were turbulent times for Judah, the southern kingdom of the divided land of Palestine. They had been threatened by the mighty Assyrians, their powerful neighbours; many of the people were in exile in Babylon. And for those who remained in Jerusalem, life was far from secure. Many of them, fearing the Assyrians, wanted to make an alliance with another powerful neighbour, Egypt. This was a small, powerless people, and it is hardly surprising that they would identify the power of God with the power of the strong surrounding states. They were not the last to think that God was on the side of the big battalions. But Isaiah did not think so. He believed that more than anything else, God was on the side of justice and righteousness. And so he prophesied.

It was no good the people of Judah looking for salvation in powerful allies. It was no good them fasting, sacrificing, praying loudly in the temple if they did not do justice to the poor, act with fairness and hospitality to the foreigner and show compassion to those who were suffering. The whole of Isaiah is a clarion-call, agonisingly pointing out the consequences of putting one's strength in idols, whether of wealth, military might or piety, rather than trusting humbly in God. And it draws a bleak picture indeed of these consequences: defeat, abandonment, death for the people of Judah.

And yet the book is also intensely humane: it holds out hope as well as judgement. It does not leave the people without encouragement, and this passage, the message of the good news of deliverance, was intended to reassure and hearten. We should be clear about these words; they were speaking of real, material circumstances, of real poverty, real captivity, real broken-heartedness. For Isaiah, these were not symbolic phrases. This is not a spiritualised prophecy; it is a testimony of God's deliverance for those who were destitute, homeless, hungry, without the means to support themselves and their families, without land. The captives in Babylon would return home, those in prison would be released. The anguish of those who were broken-hearted would come to an end. *This* is the divine manifesto Jesus chose when he announced himself as the promised one.

We are accustomed in Christianity to hearing this passage spiritualised and individualised, for its meaning to be interpreted as spiritual good news, as deliverance from our sinful selves. Clearly, there is no reason for us to reject this interpretation; the meaning of the gospel has always been fuller, more comprehensive, more paradoxical than at first seemed likely, and many accepted norms were turned on their heads; the good news was not just for Jews but also for the Gentiles, for the sinner as well as the righteous, for the individual person as well as for the whole community. But we should never forget that this manifesto which Jesus claimed as his own was as a Jew, for whom there was no salvation apart from the community, and for whom good news for the poor (by which was meant anyone who was marginalised) was exactly that – the kind of news that made a real difference.

It's a long way from that prophecy, echoing down the hundreds of years till the time of Jesus, a long way indeed to the small group of disciples still traumatised, one imagines, from their Easter experience and its aftermath. They had followed Jesus from that first occasion when he had met some of them fishing and given them a great catch, then invited them to follow him in another kind of work. They had followed him through heady, exhilarating moments of power and the rapturous welcome of the ordinary people; through moments of confusion and anxiety when they did not know where they were going, or why, or how they would get there; through moments of intimacy and deep sharing. And finally, they had followed him into danger, arrest and death by torture. Only most of them had not acquitted themselves very well when it came to the crunch. None of them had been any use: they had left him feeling quite alone, and only the women and John had been able to see it through to the end.

And then, the rumours, the appearances, the strange meetings, and they were as disquieting as they were joyful. What were they to do now? And anyway, they probably couldn't cope with it. In these strange days after Easter, confused, embarrassed, leaderless, the disciples did what most of us do when events get too much for us to handle: they ran for home, back to Galilee, away from the city and back to where it all began. And now, in a strange poetic symmetry, they were going fishing.

Then, 'It is the Lord', said the disciple Jesus loved to Peter. And Peter, eager, impulsive to the last, his instincts once again outrunning his brain, jumped into the water and headed for the shore. It was the eye of love which first recognised Jesus and named him; but it was Peter who moved. Perhaps it was this quality of Peter's, of always being the first to act, however wrongheadedly, that Jesus treasured enough to see in him the qualities of potential leadership. No theorist, Peter, but someone who, for right or wrong, committed himself to action. Jesus' judgement of him, that he would come good in the end, that he should have another chance, turned out to be sound, though fewer these days are prepared to give failure, disloyalty, betrayal even, a second chance.

Nevertheless, Jesus' followers were not what you would call promising material to carry through such a revolutionary and glorious manifesto. Young, unlearned, hard-up, few of them with any status or authority, with a track record of failure to understand and failure in faithfulness, it can have rarely have seemed so obvious to any group of people that they were the wrong ones for the job, especially given the intractable circumstances that faced them: a country occupied, divided by sectarianism, closed minds and resistance to any challenge or change to the point of idolatry. And yet a country in which the poor people went on suffering, the broken-hearted still wept, the prisons overflowed, justice was driven away and truth stumbled in the marketplace.

It is a good thing for us that we do not have to wait, as the disciples did, to know what lay ahead of them. We know about Pentecost, the coming of the Holy Spirit among the followers of Jesus to empower them, to inspire them, to make them able, to build their capacity. For surely the Spirit of the Lord of which Isaiah spoke, and which Jesus received at his baptism in the Jordan river is the same Spirit that came upon the disciples in Jerusalem. By the power of that Spirit, they understood their discipleship anew. By its power, they were able to communicate across every barrier. By that Spirit, they became exactly the people who were needed.

I suppose most churches these days have many times when their courage fails, when they too feel 'we're not the right people for the job' – we are too young, too old, too few, too weak, too whatever it is that saps our confidence. This manifesto is too great a task for us. But we need to remember that pentecostal gift. As a community of Jesus Christ, we are a community that bears within it the spirit of Isaiah, the spirit of Jesus, the spirit of God. And from Pentecost, no longer was that Spirit to be found in one person – it was a gift to the whole community, and it can only be actualised by and in and for the whole community. Paul emphasised that over and over again. The Spirit's presence is shown in some way in each person for the good of all. So in order to follow our manifesto, we need to be always looking for the gifts of everyone, because each has something unique which everyone else needs, to set free their gift, and without this mutuality, this reciprocity of Spirit, we cannot truly be the church. However able a minister, he or she is only a part of the whole, and to discern the Spirit working in our midst is the task of the whole people of God.

When I was writing these earlier words about the circumstances that faced the followers of Jesus after Easter, I could not help but think that they were remarkably similar in many ways to the circumstances of Northern Ireland today. As that place takes tentative moves towards, if not yet the good news of which Isaiah speaks, at least better news, moves for which we all pray, I am conscious once again that we here, and in every church in the world, are one in the Spirit with them by virtue of Pentecost. Our calling to be the church takes different forms; and theirs, in the search for a just peace after so much hurt, is a demanding one indeed. Every day, Christians in Northern Ireland must feel, 'we are not the right people for the job'. Perhaps our solidarity with them should be not just in our prayers, but in our constant affirmation that we are not called to be the church in our own strength, but in the power of the Spirit of Isaiah, the Spirit of Jesus, the Spirit of God – and that that Spirit lives in the *whole* people of God *for* the whole people of God.

For the 'preaching-in' of Rev. Peter Macdonald, St George's West, Edinburgh, 26 April 1998.

Testimony Stoops
to Mother Tongue

(Genesis 11, 1–9, Acts 2, 1–21)

*'Let us go down and mix up their language so that they will not
understand one another.' (Genesis 11, 7)*
*'All of us hear them speaking in our own languages about the
great things that God has done.' (Acts 2, 11)*

There is a wonderful line in Robert Browning's long poem, *The
Ring and the Book*, '... *when testimony stooped to mother tongue.*'
Testimony stoops to mother tongue. Immediately, I have a vivid
picture of a mother bending down to her small child playing on the
floor, and talking to her in that beautiful language which people,
especially their parents but others as well, use with babies and little
children, that mixture of words and soft gurgling sounds which is
somewhere between speech and song, but always sounds encouraging
and soothing and playful all at once. We laugh at it, call it *baby-talk*, but
actually we know that it is both how we make small children feel safe
and loved, *and* that it is through these sounds that we ourselves first
learned to communicate. It's not a language that can be spoken from
a great height: you have to get alongside the child to be close, to be
heard. You have to stoop.

English is my native language. We who are native English
speakers are pretty lucky, for it is a language which is widely spoken;
mostly, it should be said, because of our colonial history. We can visit
large parts of the globe and find that almost everyone has at least basic

English, far more knowledge than we do of their languages. It helps us to get around, to make ourselves understood, to communicate. There are clearly great advantages in having languages which extend beyond national borders, as Greek did in the time of Christ, as Latin did in the Middle Ages.

A few years ago, I spent some time working as a locum minister for the English-speaking congregation of the Presbyterian church on the Indian Ocean island of Mauritius. Now Mauritius is a fascinating multi-cultural place. The official language is English, from a time when Britain was the colonial power. It's used in the Parliament, in the law courts, by the police. But the language of the education system, of the middle classes, of polite society, is French. And the language of the people, of the streets, is Creole, a mixture of French and African languages. And for most people, there is yet another language, the language of home, of their own culture, which might be Hindi, Urdu or Cantonese. It is a pentecostal island.

Though my church was technically Presbyterian, in actual fact it was thoroughly ecumenical, because it was the only English-speaking worship on this island of a million people. So there were also Baptists and Methodists, Anglicans and Catholics, a Christian Scientist, a Jain, even a few Hindus there with Christian spouses. Many were expatriates, and they came from Australia and Indonesia, from India and Sri Lanka, and from a dozen African countries. What they had in common was the desire to worship in English. It was wonderful to share worship with such a richly diverse group of people. The English language was our common ground, and it was the thing which broke down other barriers of culture, nationality and denomination. But for the great majority of them, it was not their mother tongue. For the Mauritians, who were the heart of the congregation, English was their third or even their fourth language. So, though it was a common tongue, and a means of sharing and communication, it was not the language of testimony.

Testimony is an important word for Christians. It comes from the Latin word, *testis,* from which we also get the word testament, and it means witness. Now, I don't imagine I have anything to tell Methodists about testimony, bearing witness. I remember as a young divinity student being tremendously impressed by John Wesley's dictum that a Christian had to be ready to preach, pray or die at any minute. It was a standard of absolute clarity and demand. And to bear witness is at the heart of Christian discipleship. It is to tell *our* story, from *our* experience, to say, not just, this is what it means, this is how it is, which is abstract and theoretical, but, this is what it means for *me*, this is how it is for *me*. As Max Boyce, the Welsh comedian, used to say, 'I know, 'cos I was there!'

But to tell our story, to give our testimony, is a deep thing. Because then we are talking about something very important, very significant to us. This happened, and this is how it affected me, how it changed me. Perhaps we fell in love, and nothing was ever the same again. Perhaps we had a baby and nothing was ever the same again. Perhaps someone we loved very much died and nothing was ever the same again. Perhaps we endured great suffering, and nothing was ever the same again. We try to describe the most profound human experiences and emotions – and we find ourselves struggling to express them, perhaps even lost for words. When we are bearing witness, giving testimony, an unfamiliar language will not do. We need a language of the heart; we need a mother tongue. We are bringing out things that are precious, fragile, intimate. We are opening our hearts.

And although English is my native language, I would not describe it as my mother tongue. Mother tongue for me is the language of poetry and song and story. Perhaps I have been shaped in this by the songs my mother used to sing to me when I was little, by the poems and stories my grandmother told me. Or perhaps by the poetry of the Bible and the hymns, especially the old Irish and Scottish ones I grew up singing in church. I just know that when I want to express something very dear, very important to me, my deepest loves, my deepest sorrows, my fondest hopes, that is the language that comes naturally to me. And other people too, have their own mother tongues. For some, it is the language of science, or even of mathematics. It is a source of great mystery and wonder to me that there are people in the world for whom the poetry of numbers expresses more fully and beautifully than anything else who they are and what matters to them.

Sometimes people use a mother tongue that may seem at first to be quite trivial and even silly to express what is important to them. I think that sometimes the language of football, for example, can be a mother tongue. People who are inarticulate in every other regard can suddenly come alive, can suddenly speak the language of belonging, of loyalty through bad times and good, of appreciation of beauty and skill, of hope for a new start, another chance next week, next season or whenever.

And sometimes the mother tongue is not words at all: sometimes it is music or painting, dance or gardening, anything by which we express what is most important to us, what it means for us, how it changes us. We don't always bear witness best through our words. I remember my mother once saying to me ruefully:

> *If I waited for your father to tell me he loves me, I'd have to wait for ever. But I just believe that he does because he takes the rubbish down for me and brings me breakfast in bed every day.*

We're all familiar with the mother tongue of practical, loving care, even if we sometimes take it for granted and forget that it *is* a language, a way of communicating. In the whole long history of the Christian church, it has probably been the most used, and the most effective form of testimony, the simple witness of loving one's neighbour, whom you can see, for the sake of loving God, whom you can't see. But that whole long history only exists at all because of testimony. The church *is* the heartwrenching testimony of Mary in the garden, meeting the risen Jesus and being told to go and tell the others; it is the mother tongue of Peter, stumbling in shame and then walking on the water; it is of Thomas, not trusting to words or sight but needing to touch. It is the gospel writers, each with his own mother tongue: Matthew, the legalist; Mark, writing with all the immediacy of journalism; Luke, the doctor with his healing stories; and John, the poet-mystic. It is the passionate and often intemperate letters of Paul, but more than that, it is that he went on and on putting not just his words but his body on the line.

And then it is the slaves and martyrs who gave their testimony in the blood circuses of Rome. It is the Celts with their great journeys and their great art, the Benedictines with their mother tongue of hospitality and prayer; it is Francis, getting down off his horse to kiss the leper and being utterly changed; it is Martin Luther, wrestling long years of fear and self-disgust and then suddenly having his mother tongue loosened by the experience of grace. It is the preaching of John and the hymns of Charles. It is the fire of justice of a Shaftesbury or a Martin Luther King. It is the care of a Teresa. It is the courage of a Romero speaking out against oppression even while knowing that his life was in great danger, shot dead while saying Mass. So many witnesses, so many mother tongues stooping to testimony, getting down, getting alongside people to share the story of how they had been changed.

So important has testimony been for people of faith that it's quite astonishing when we read in the book of Genesis that God seems to have objected to people understanding one another. Remember the passage we heard: *'Let us go down and mix up their language so that they will not understand one another'*, the Lord said. How peculiar! Not to want people to understand one another? How thoroughly unpleasant this makes God seem. Surely communication is so important that anything that helps it must be a good thing. If only people spoke the same language of the heart, understood one another, then wouldn't so many of their problems, their arguments, their wars even, come to an end. There might be no Bosnia, no Middle East, no

Northern Ireland, if only people could communicate. And since the passage seems to suggest that the Lord put an end to understanding simply so that he could keep them under his thumb, it makes the Lord seem even more petty. What are we to make of this passage?

Well of course, on one level, we can explain it by saying that the ancient, nomadic peasant people who collected the writings that make up the book of Genesis were simply giving their best shot to the vexed question of explaining *why* there were all these different peoples in the world, and why they all spoke different languages. The explanation they came up with is just a wonderful imaginative story. And it is. But we should not let that make us overlook the deep spiritual truth that is also contained in the story. Because the fact is, having a common language, even having a shared mother tongue is not enough to bring about a world of justice, love and peace. Understanding itself is not enough. We only have to look at the world around us to see that.

Because we live in a time of unparalleled mass communication. Far from not understanding one another, we can communicate at the flick of a switch, or the click of a mouse on a computer. It's not just English that has become a global language. We can access information on an enormous scale through the Internet; we can move money around the globe in seconds: 40 million transactions an hour in the stock exchanges of the world. And we can see what's happening in Rwanda or Indonesia or the Sudan on our television screens *as it's happening*. Now we are all witnesses. We cannot any longer plead ignorance. We understand all right.

But we can understand, and still not be changed. And in the Christian story, it's not the witnessing, it's not the believing, it's not even the understanding that's the most important thing. It's the being changed into doing things differently. It's the being there, and then it's what happened next! Remember what happened to the followers of Jesus. They witnessed his death. They were there, or, at least, thereabouts. Then, in an at first incredulous and then rather confused fashion, they witnessed the resurrection. They were there. Against all the odds, they began to believe. But still they didn't understand. Then, gradually, they began to understand a little bit better. So what did they do next. Well actually, not a lot. They shuffled about between Galilee and Jerusalem. They prayed a lot. They held meetings. Who can blame them? We would have done the same, probably. They were confused; they didn't know what was expected of them; they were probably scared to tell their story.

And then Pentecost came, the day we celebrate *this* day, and everything changed. They got the Spirit, it came upon them like wind and fire, and they could talk to everyone. They found a heart language for people from everywhere. This was a form of communication that went far deeper than simply having a common language, simply understanding. This was a language that *moved* people to the depths of their being, that changed them in their hearts and their lives. When we read further on into that same chapter in Acts, we find that the lives of the believers were dramatically changed. They continued in close fellowship; they shared their belongings; they redistributed their money to those in need; they ate together in their homes; they worshipped together; they were at peace with each other; and *they were joyful*. To use a modern image, the disciples after the resurrection were like people who had won the Lottery, but had never cashed the cheque. Now at Pentecost they finally came into their inheritance: the power of the Holy Spirit to set them free from the arrogance and greed and egotism of Babylon, and to change their lives.

People who are native English speakers can get very lazy, arrogant even. We can think that speaking loudly is the same as communication, and that hearing is the same as understanding, and that knowing is the same as acting. But it's not. The Spirit that moved people at Pentecost spoke many mother tongues; but it was the message that inspired them, not the medium, the message of forgiveness and hope and reconciliation and new beginnings, the message of changed lives. The testimony of the disciples made sense now!

For us today, seeking our Pentecost, perhaps we need to remember, as the people of Northern Ireland undoubtedly do, that all our words and all our promises are not pentecostal unless they lead to changed lives – a change that listens as well as speaks, that tries painfully to learn another person's mother tongue instead of assuming that they must speak ours, that moves towards another instead of waiting for them to come to us, that puts aside its dreams of towers in the sky for the sake of peace and justice on the ground, that bears witness not to our own self-interest, but to the life and death and resurrection of Jesus Christ, that lives in close fellowship and shares of its substance with people in need. For me, I want to say that I see a greater pentecostal testimony in 60,000 people linking arms in Birmingham to urge for the cancellation of the murderous debt of the world's poorest people than in the most advanced tele-evangelism. I truly believe that for millions, such a cancellation would communicate better than any words, so that they could say with joy, 'all of us hear them speaking in our own languages about the great things God has done.'

> *Spirit of truth, whom the world can never grasp, touch our hearts*
> *with the shock of your coming; fill us with the desire for your*
> *disturbing peace and fire us with longing to speak your word which*
> *cannot be contained. Through Jesus Christ, Amen. (Janet Morley)*

Faces of God

God the Mother
(John 3, 1–8)

I used to have a poster of a big daisy opening to the sun, with a quotation from Bob Dylan on it *'S/he who's not busy being born is busy dying.'* I guess it was a reminder that all the time we're surrounded by opportunities for growth, for new life, for being born into new knowledge, new responsibilities, new life. We tend to think of ourselves more as people who *give birth*, who are creative, whether it's to children, or to an idea or talent, people who make a garden, a painting, a programme, a friendship, and who nurture these. But with every day, with every change in our lives, God is still creating *us*. I remember thinking with not a little panic after the birth of my first child, 'How will I cope, being a new-born mother?'

In John's gospel, Jesus speaks of the necessity for us to be born again of water and of the spirit, but I think that the Spirit of God goes on creating us anew – another poster I saw said *'Be patient with me … God isn't finished with me yet.'* Our full potential, our true self, is only really known by God. Our birth struggle – and it is a struggle – is to get our little egotistical selves out of the way, and let God's spirit bring forth our truer, fuller, more human selves; and the womb in which our true selves are formed is our relationship with our neighbours. A wise Jew once said, 'It is not given to human beings to begin – but it is given to them to begin again!'

Because She Cares

Each day
God the Mother walks with me.

She holds my hand
at busy crossroads,
reminds me to be careful
because it matters to her
what happens to me.

She points out rainbows
when my mind is busy
on the deluge of paperwork
impatient on my desk.

She smiles at me
through friendly eyes
and with a blackbird's song.

God the Mother
walks with me
and my heart skips along.   *(Nancy Somerville)*

God the Wrestler
(Genesis 32, 22–32)

Like Jacob, we too seek to bend God to our will, to remake the world to our own design. Sometimes we do it arrogantly, carelessly, not attentive to the needs and hopes of others. Sometimes we are relentlessly self-pitying. Sometimes we're just too caught up in our own little world. It's what the ancient Greeks called *hubris*, and it always went before a fall. But sometimes a fall's not such a bad thing; sometimes it's the only way we will abandon ourselves to *real* trust, to being caught up in the arms of God, and give up our illusion of control and self-sufficiency. Jacob had to fall and be wounded before he received the blessing of God. And it has been the case in every time and culture that it has been the poor and defenceless whose trust in God has been the most marked; those people whose powerlessness has meant they have no illusions of control.

It's hard to bend ourselves to God's will if we never relax, soften, trust. Trust is so much more than just intellectual assent to a set of beliefs. We trust with our hearts, or even our gut, not just our head. Wrestling with God invites us to struggle – but it also invites us to a surrender in which we find holding and blessing and peace.

Credo

Today has been a restless day
things going wrong in all directions
and my anger rising
at others
at my circumstances
at myself.

God, you are in the midst of this
I sense your presence
prowling like a tiger
pushing me
pursuing me
restless yourself until I change

I am ready to let rip
to hurl stones into oceans
to pound my fists into a brick wall

I am ready to shout
to rip sheets into shreds
to curse the darkness
to bury my head into warm flesh and sob.

I am afraid, God
that there is no one here but you and me
my friends are out or busy or far away.
Do I trust you enough to give you my anger, my loneliness?
Do I believe you enough to reach through the emptiness
and grasp for your hand?

Credo
God, I love you,
I can say no other words.   (Ruth Burgess)

God the Weeper
(John 11, 28–37)

There is nothing to compare with the pain of death.
You were here, and now you are not. That's all.
I search for you in old photographs, letters, things you touched,
things that remind me of you,
but they cannot fill the space you occupied.

Sometimes I think we Christians place burdens on ourselves which are intolerable, inhuman, even, in our thinking about suffering and sorrow. We feel we must be stoic, strong, even cheerfully resigned because we are the ones who have the answer to all sadness and loss. 'Gone to a better place', 'all suffering over', 'all passion spent'. In reality, death strips us naked, shatters our world, disintegrates our identity, whatever kind of death it is. Its pain is huge. In reality, we have a passion for living, a desire to see good times – but it seems kind of disloyal to say so.

But it is this very desire for life that God loves in us; it is our happiness that is also God's happiness, our sorrows God's sorrows. So much does God love our desire for life that Jesus suffered our death to bring us new life. It is *life* that God desires for us. It was over the tragedy and pity and beauty and love of life that Jesus wept – for his beloved city, for his beloved friend. To be human is to mourn in the face of death; and we do not surrender our own lives lightly to death. But to be a follower of Jesus is to have surrendered our lives *anyway*, not to death but to the love of God, which is not limited by time or space or mortality. When I was younger, and knew George MacLeod, one of his thrilling but daunting attributes was to say the most extraordinary things in ordinary conversations. He would come up and ask you if you loved your enemies, and did good to those who hated you! He would tell us that through our baptism, we were already dead, and our lives were hidden in Christ with God. It was very disconcerting having someone say things like that outside a church. He would say that, for us, the undertaker had been and gone.

In my pilgrimage, I increasingly find that things like birth and death get confused – or rather, that they are completely tied up together; as we die to our old selves, we are born to new ones ... in the midst of life, we are in death – or is it the other way round? The life and death of Columba are tied up with my life – if it wasn't for him, I wouldn't be standing here in *this* here and now, in this way – and also with my death. Though he didn't know it, Columba witnessed to *me*, not of death, but of the love of God for life, including mine, through and beyond death. 'It is not given to us to begin – but it is given to us to begin again.' *'Unless a grain of seed falls into the ground ...' (John 12, 24).*

> *Lord, help us to see in the groaning of creation not death throes but birth pangs; help us to see in suffering a promise for the future, because it is a cry against the inhumanity of the present. Help us to glimpse in protest the dawn of justice, in the Cross the pathway to resurrection, and in suffering the seeds of joy. (Rubem Alves)*

The Soft Whisper
of a Voice

(1 Kings 19, 1–15, Galatians 3, 23–29, Luke 8, 26–39)

*Then the Lord sent a furious wind that split
the hills and shattered the rock – but the Lord was not in the wind.
The wind stopped blowing, and then there was an earthquake –
but the Lord was not in the earthquake. After the earthquake, there
was a fire – but the Lord was not in the fire. And after the fire,
there was the soft whisper of a voice.*
(1 Kings 19, 11–12)

This is a day to celebrate beauty and fruitfulness and creativity. We are so thankful for warmer weather, and the promise for many of us of holidays to come. We are so thankful for the long days of light and for the sunshine, touching us like a blessing, melting away our disgruntledness and making our disagreements somehow less significant. There are few black moods that cannot be improved by half an hour wandering in the park or lounging in a garden like a cat uncurling on warm stones to make the most of late afternoon sunshine. We who live in cold northern climes yearn towards midsummer and the light evenings that are our compensation for murky, miserable winters. There is an ancient Celtic legend that on Easter Day the sun itself danced for joy, and we are poor souls indeed if we cannot catch our breath in delight at what the Orcadian poet George MacKay Brown described so beautifully 'a lark splurges in galilees of sky'.

Or if we cannot take pleasure in the infinite beauty of flowers, their variety, their subtlety of colour and scent, their capacity to stir our memories and awaken us to delight. There's a wonderful bit in the book *The Color Purple* by the American writer Alice Walker, which talks about how God gets miserable when people walk past the colour purple in a field without even noticing, because God is always trying to please us.

I find that even the rain is more bearable in the summer, when one is not at the same time bracing oneself against the biting wind of a dreich day; on the street that I walk along to go home, it drips loudly off tall horse-chestnut trees and copper beeches, and elder and hawthorn bushes lush in their greenness, and you can smell dust and earth and blossom, even in the middle of the city. Summer brings us to our senses, we are arrested by sight and smell and the touch of overhanging foliage and the sound of birds singing. Truly it is a time to give thanks for the promise of spring once again fulfilled, for the human care and skill that helps it to come to fullness, and for the goodness of God in creation.

So it is that the two stories from the Bible that we heard read strike a discordant note in the midst of the song of summer. Strange, dark unsettling stories, both of them: the Old Testament account of the prophet Elijah, persecuted, afraid, alone, fleeing for his life into the wilderness; and the gospel story of the man driven by his demons out of the town, out of human community, out of his mind till the only place left for him was the cemetery. Grim stories, both of them, because they name things most of us would rather not think about – persecution, madness – and yet curiously similar, which is presumably why the lectionary links them.

Both of them are about men who have been pushed to the very edge of existence, out beyond all ordinary life. Neither has gone by free choice: Elijah, under sentence of death for leading a popular revolt against the cruel and oppressive regime of Ahab and Jezebel, has been abandoned by the people. All his fellow prophets have been killed, and he is utterly isolated, a danger to any who would even think of assisting him.

And the other is suffering from an extremity of mental

disturbance which means he has broken through all of the boundaries that usually constrain human beings. His behaviour has broken all the codes of acceptability. He has broken his ties to home and community. He had stripped off his clothes, that last vestige of protection, and roams naked, beyond all care for what others think of him. We are told that he had even broken the chains that had been put round his hands and feet to bind him, presumably by the townsfolk either for his own or for their protection. He too is an outcast, a pariah. For both of them, the only boundary they have not crossed is the one between life and death.

And both men have in common that they arouse fear in the minds of the people around them; not only the ones to whom they pose a threat, whether real or imagined, but also the ones who simply don't want them around, don't want to have to think about them, don't want the contagion of persecution or madness to stick to them.

It is quite possible to read these stories as history: interesting, but detached from our modern experience. A biblical prophet of over 3000 years ago, contending with primitive warring tribes. And an almost equally distant unfortunate in a time when demon possession was a common occurrence, and cures were only ever miraculous.

But if we are honest, we recognise that the experience of persecution by cruel and despotic rulers is still with us in the world, and that those who speak out against tyranny and injustice are just as likely to find themselves targeted, isolated and betrayed, are as likely as Elijah to find themselves alone in the wilderness. This is, after all, the same world in which a Catholic bishop was murdered in Guatemala a few weeks ago for a trenchant human-rights report which named killers in the security forces still to be brought to justice, in which Aung San Suu Kyi is still under house arrest in Burma after years of separation from her family, in which Mordecai Vanunu is still in solitary confinement in an Israeli jail for telling the world of his country's nuclear capability, a secret widely known – and these are only the ones we hear about. There are still plenty of people living in the extremity of persecution like Elijah.

But a good deal closer to home, there are plenty of people whose inner conflicts and compulsions drive them, tear their lives apart, render them anguished and alone. The world recognises to some extent the isolation of its heroes and prophets, even if it doesn't want to get too close, but the distress of mental illness is still exacerbated for many people by a society that would prefer they were invisible, that stigmatises them, yes, that even demonises them.

For, if the truth be told, we all have a demon or two, do we not? The nasty habit we cannot break, the night fear that we cannot shake off, the shameful moment from our past that still makes us break out in a cold sweat when we remember it. We who are well-adjusted, functioning, respectable, have our sleeping demons well under control. We do not appreciate having them kicked awake by being confronted by someone in whom they are unconcealed. It is simply too unpleasant, too disturbing of our good image of ourselves. After all, we could not possibly be like them, perish the thought. We want them where we cannot see them. And sometimes, if we do see them, we will go to great lengths to get them to go away, to get rid of them. We will demand that they be removed, forcibly if necessary. Or we will project our own demons on to them; after all, a few more won't make any difference to them!

> *My daughter dreams of spiders,*
> *shakes with fear, becomes hysterical.*
> *In the daytime, one in her room*
> *has much the same effect as nightmare.*
> *No spider has ever hurt her.*
> *But other things have.*
> *Black, huge scary spiders become the carriers*
> *of all her agonies and anxieties.*
> *In my mind, I understand this reasonable explanation.*
> *In my heart, I am distressed to see her so possessed.*

Well, spiders are relatively harmless things to demonise. Other demonisation causes more damage. People of a different ethnic origin or colour are demonised. People whose sexual orientation, or religion, or culture, is different are demonised. Homeless people are routinely attacked and beaten up. These are people with practically *nothing*. Like spiders, they pose no threat, we just don't like the look of them. And people who are mentally ill are demonised. Often, they are made into scapegoats.

> *Did he hold the people's fears?*
> *Did he carry their sins?*
> *And did the weight crush every form and structure in him*
> *for the containment and direction of his passions,*
> *or did he never have them?*
> *He tore apart the chains that bound him,*
> *loosening the furies to rage in all directions,*
> *damaging most of all himself.*
> *There are children like him in our country.*

It is a curious thing that the world feels it necessary to attack people who are already outside the comfort zone of belonging.

> *I live on the edge*
> *of madness.*
> *Only a membrane*
> *fine as silk*
> *weaves between my self*
> *and inner caves*
> *where pain and terror lurk.*   (Kay Carmichael)

Can we imagine what it's like to live so close to these inner caves, what it's like to live where nothing in your life is the least bit reliable, including your own thoughts, where each day only offers more chaos, where every time you go out you are marked as different, an outsider, not one of us, in ways you cannot eradicate? Well, perhaps we can. The woman who wrote these lines is a successful professional woman – but she has the courage to confront her own inner demons, and to name the fact that she is not different. Because it takes courage to risk associating ourselves with anything, or anyone, that the world counts a failure, whom it sees as a loser in the great lottery of modern life.

We know from the accounts of the same story in the other Synoptic gospels, for it is told in all three of them that the man driven by demons wandered among the hills and the tombs, screaming, and cutting himself. Cutting oneself, self-mutilation, is a not uncommon practice among people whose mental distress is so great that to feel actual physical pain, even if self-inflicted, is actually some relief. At least it's a pain you can put a name to, a way of trying to externalise what's really an interior agony. And we do not know what were the factors in this man's life that led him to such a tormented state. We do know that he described his demons as legion, the name for a regiment of Roman soldiers, because there were so many of them, and we are reminded that he lived in an occupied territory. We are familiar with the huge traumas occupation can cause from our own times. Personal, family and political pressures no doubt all played their part, as they do in most human suffering.

And we know that Elijah too lived in a time of great social and political pressures: war, drought, famine, oppression. You could say that the only difference between these two men was that the one was torn apart by his demons, while the other confronted them, challenged them and held firm against their onslaught. Perhaps the prophetic task God had called Elijah to allowed him to direct his demons in a creative way. Who knows – but it's a thin line of difference, isn't it, and which of us could say with conviction which side of the line we would find ourselves on in the face of such pressures? The Bible tells us about a lot of people on the thin line: some, like Moses, came down on one side; others, like David, on the other. Jesus came down on one side,

Peter on the other. But whether they disintegrated in the face of their demons, or whether they maintained their integrity, they all ended up in a wilderness somewhere, alone, abandoned, despairing.

Excluded from culture, from their human community, the delights of nature were no compensation to them either. Both these stories have in common their encounter with the forces of nature in their most savage, least benign forms. The story of the man with demons is actually preceded in all the gospels with the story of Jesus stilling the storm which threatened to drown the disciples in their boat. The inference is unavoidable. First Jesus calms the storm on the lake, *and then*, as he is actually stepping ashore, he meets the man and calms the storm in his soul, which is, in effect, threatening to destroy him with its ferocity. He has the authority to calm *every* kind of storm.

And in Elijah's encounter with the Lord in the cave, he is sent out on to the open mountaintop. First there is a hurricane. Then there is an earthquake. Then there is a fire. We are left in no doubt that the forces of nature are in the power of God, who sent the wind and the earthquake and the fire. This is nature implacable, capable of destruction as well as creation. *But the Lord was not in them.* Elijah must wait, cowering and terrified as he might well be, to find the way God comes to human beings. And *then* the Lord came … in the soft whisper of a voice.

Both to Elijah on the mountain, and to the tormented man among the graves, the divine voice is not heard in the ferocity of a raging wind. It is not heard in the growl and rumble of an earthquake. It is not heard in the heat of an all-consuming fire. It is heard in what the great hymn calls 'the still, small voice of calm'. Laying aside power, God comes gently, reassuringly, with hope, a new task to do and the promise of companions to Elijah. Laying aside power, God comes in Jesus to the man among the graves, drawing him back into life, back into human community with a task to do, letting the demons go gently into the Palestinian equivalent of spiders:

Sometimes you have to release the demonic spirits,
let them go in the least destructive way,
loving them as they go.
In different circumstances,
they could have been angels.

The soft whisper of a voice. Is this not the way grace comes? When we are in the midst of the storm, we do not even notice more thundering. We are not so different from the man driven by demons. And we are not even so different from Elijah, standing against idolatry and injustice; we too have our moments when we do more than we think we are capable of. One way or the other, we wander here or there, and we are not so different. The epistle reading for today, which we didn't hear, is from Galatians. In it, Paul reminds us that now there is no difference between Jews and gentiles, between slaves and free, between men and women – between prophets and madmen! – for we are all one in Christ Jesus. And because we share the promise, we also share the responsibility.

And so, as we enjoy the summer and take delight in its fruitfulness and leisure, we remember those who live in dark times, with clouded skies and wilderness landscapes. And we know that God is not in the wind of prejudice and self-righteousness; God is not in the rumble of ignorance and condemnation; God is not in the fire of violence and hatred. God is in the still, small voice of calm.

Speaking of Mary

(Luke 1, 46–55)

I want to begin by thanking you for inviting me to preach here in St Mary's, where I've had the chance to get to know many of you. When I came to live in Glasgow, the very first person at my door with words of welcome was a member of this church. And thank you too for the opportunity to reflect a little on the person and place of Mary of Nazareth, Mary the mother of Jesus. When I began to prepare this sermon, it struck me rather forcibly that although I have preached and written about many of the women of both Old and New Testaments, I had never preached about Mary. This could, of course, be attributed to my being a Scottish Presbyterian, a tradition which mostly makes it very clear that we pay Mary exactly the attention due to a young Jewish girl who happened to give birth to Jesus, and was obviously a very good Christian woman who suffered a lot and did her duty, but no more. Rather like one of those exemplary ministers' wives or Presidents of the Woman's Guild, in fact, and we'll say no more just now about anything mysterious or peculiar in her life, because that might be embarrassing. And perhaps some of that is the reason – but I think there are others, which I'll come back to.

So I come to preach about Mary for the first time – and at once, I am faced with the question, *which* Mary? There are so many. There is, for example, the Mary of what we might call sociological study – the young, pregnant unmarried girl, with a fantastical story of how she came about her interesting condition; the focus of adolescent self-assertion; the woman whose family demands were rejected by her son; the mother who had to watch her child executed as a condemned criminal. History and sociology are full of such women – they're usually seen as a problem. Perhaps today she might have a social worker.

Then there is the Mary of the psyche, bearer of great burdens. Mary the feminine principle in humankind, Mary the object of devotion and courtly adoration – Queen of Heaven, Queen of Hearts, Star of the Sea, Our Lady, *our* lady, of many things and places. There is Mary the perpetual virgin, symbol of purity, the good side of the virgin/harlot split. And there is Mary the Great Mother, the good mother, everybody's ideal mother – not smothering and devouring like so many of the classical Greek mothers, or treacherous and self-willed like Eve, but gentle, infinitely kind, infinitely understanding. Powerful symbols, all of these, and remarkably enduring.

For modern people too, Mary has many faces. For the poor of liberation movements in Latin America, for example, there is the prophetic Mary, symbol of closeness and accessibility, the one who understands their hope and suffering, who whispers for them into the ear of her son in heaven, Mary the mother of the mothers of the disappeared, the Mary of the Magnificat, hurling down the mighty from their thrones and lifting up the lowly. This Mary is a woman of the people, identifying with the pain of the children.

But for many women, Mary is a symbol of oppression, the bane of women's lives. She is used as the justification of doormat theology (the kind where you get to say thank you for the privilege of being trodden on) and, ostensibly, as the model of *all* human response to God of humility and servanthood, which seems to many to have been used to entrench female passivity and subjugation. And she represents for many more an impossible ideal of perfect motherhood. But perhaps most difficult of all, for many women, Mary is a denial of female sexuality. For those of us who find neither perfect virginity nor perfect motherhood possible or even desirable, a woman who combines both seems unnatural and unattractive. And to have her held up as the model of womanhood can be a deeply offensive thing that seems to require of us that we spend our whole lives denying our God-given natures. You can tell by now, I expect, that my failure to engage with Mary to date comes from somewhere deeper than my Presbyterianism.

But I don't want to get stuck there. If Mary has been the object of huge human projection and idealisation, more, perhaps, even than Jesus, and if people have made of her what it suited them to have her be, both for good and ill, then I recognise that my reaction is not really to Mary, but to the dehumanising that has been done in her name, and particularly to women. Behind all the images is a woman waiting to be discovered, and, in my particular discovery, all *my* own biases and wishes will be present, as they are in all preaching. In trying to make both you and myself aware of these, I am nevertheless not apologising for them. We all of us only ever meet God and reflect on our faith from within our own particular context and experience. God surprises us and stretches us in these exchanges. They are where the word becomes flesh for us, just as long as we remember that they are neither the only word nor the last word, but, rather, words of testimony.

When I go back to the Bible, therefore, is there a Mary I can meet with confidence? What can I know of this woman, who has carried so much in Christian history? I have to say that for me, Mary is largely unknowable, hidden from me as Mary of Nazareth by huge distances of history and geography, of culture and religion (she was, after all, a Jewish woman), by interpretation and speculation. What I have are glimpses, flashes, intimations of a flesh-and-blood woman who lived through extraordinary events.

I see that she was a woman who even at a fairly young age was the subject and not the object of her own life, who had the courage and the confidence and the inner conviction to make her own choices freely, and to assume responsibility for the consequences. She did not say, 'I'll just have to ask my father and mother, or my fiancé' as a well-brought-up Jewish girl should. She said, 'I am the Lord's servant. May it happen to me as you have said.' She said 'I', in the knowledge that she was setting in motion a train of events that might mean shame, rejection, isolation and possibly even stoning, as well as hurt to those she loved.

I see that she was a woman who thought deeply, and had the capacity to reflect on the activity of God in the life of her people and in her own life. That is to say, without ever going near a university, she was a theologian.

I see that she was a woman who sometimes got it wrong, who had to learn from her children, who needed the support of other people.

I see that she was a woman who recognised her own fears and doubt, but who chose to act out of a trust in God which led her on to strange and difficult roads – into exile, on to the way of the cross, and eventually into the first Christian fellowship.

I see that she was a woman to whom it was given to challenge values of family, culture and religion – scandalously pregnant with a nameless child, married to a husband who was not the father of her child, mother to a man who was not her son. She was the cornerstone of the new community whose belonging comes from love and not biology.

What I see can only be discerned from what she did, how she acted. All else is in the realm of interpretation, dogma and imagination. My understanding of Mary, therefore, is that she was a woman who above all else participated in birth, in many kinds of birth, in the birth of the new, and that birth perhaps also came as a kind of death.

And it seems to me that as people who have been born again into the community of God's love, and who desire to be part of God's new creation, the challenge of Mary to us is not what we speculate about her character, but whether we are able to be active participants, as she was, in the many kinds of births God invites us to, those births by which, as Paul says, our whole being will be set free.

And in these births we take many parts, as Mary did. What does it mean for us, women and men both, to be virgin in a way that includes but also goes beyond our sexuality to transcend a technical description? Does it mean something like opening ourselves to the movements of the Holy Spirit in the deepest and most intimate places of our hearts and lives to the conception of something quite new – a new idea, a new commitment, a new challenge, a new love?

And what does it mean for us, women and men both, to be motherly, to allow the new creation time for gestation, to wait, aware and attentive to the new life growing within us, hard waiting that often becomes weary and even despairing, wanting to get rid of this new burden, to shake it off and return to the carefree days of the past, yet awed and curious to see its face and form? And then to labour, to enter willingly into the pain of giving birth, to give our strength and our co-operation as the life that wills to be born when the time is right ripples and surges painfully through us.

And what does it mean for us, women and men both, to be fatherly, creating conditions for growth, conditions of security, care, steadfastness, to be the shoulder to lean on and the arm that steadies?

And what does it mean for us, women and men both, to be the midwife? The one, who for the sake of the new life to come, encourages, soothes, exhorts and reassures, and goes on doing it when the father worries and the mother grows faint and the child is slow in coming, and who will take the strain when the moment is near and draw the child triumphantly into life.

And what does it mean for us, women and men both, to be the one coming to new birth – pushing our way down the dark tunnel of the unknown, leaving the security of the womb of the past, the known, the familiar, to be born again a new creation, breaking the cord that binds us to a smaller, more restricted life, free to live a new fullness of life? Not just one birth but many births – or rather perhaps the birth of new parts of us – the birth of new hope in us, the birth of new love in us, the birth of new ability in us, the birth of new wonder in us.

As for Mary, there is no easy way to new life. The risks are there, the pain is real, the labour long. In *her* human life, we see the pattern of our lives and the divine activity within them – God as lover, as father, as mother, God as child, God as midwife. And I find that in the woman Mary, it is enough for me to see one who, in the deepest and freest and most courageous trust, said 'yes' to the pain and the joy and the challenge of the new. And for that I give thanks, and hear again the invitation to me to the miracle and mystery of embodying God's love and God's creativity, always beginning right here and now.

After the War is Over

(Luke 15, 11–32)

L ast week, in one of the places I work, I was talking to an old man about his life, including his lifelong involvement in the church. Most of his memories were happy, contented ones – he had the tolerance and wisdom that often comes with age – but his face clouded over when the conversation touched on the war. 'There are things I did,' he said painfully, 'I can't forgive myself for them.'

This week, I went to see *Braveheart*, a stirring if somewhat fanciful film. But there's one scene in it, before a bloody battle, in which the soldiers are being forgiven in advance for whatever crimes they might commit on the battlefield. Remembrance Sunday seems an appropriate time to think about what it means to forgive ourselves. As we honour courage and heroism, as we remember the horrors of fascism and genocide, it is still the hardest question to ask. Being on the winning side, even the justice of the cause, cannot take away that question, 'What does it mean to forgive myself?' Because war is fought on the basis of the ends justifying the means, all other considerations have to be ruthlessly excluded for the purpose of achieving the ends. But after the war is over, the question of the means used to achieve these ends seeps back into the soul.

Most of us have not had to face the extremities of war. But the awareness of failure, of hurting others deeply, of moments of profound self-disgust, may haunt us just as much. I can never forget the anguished cry of a young woman after listening to an eloquent sermon on God's acceptance of us: *'but I can't accept my acceptance'*.

Stories like these make me somewhat impatient with tabloid

journalists who gather like vultures after disasters or tragic crimes asking, do you forgive them, do you forgive them? They reduce what is one of the most difficult and yet most liberating aspects of human experience to a trite and nasty formula. They confuse the intention with the action. It's a bit like saying, 'They had a very nice wedding, so they lived happily ever after.'

In order to face what it means to forgive ourselves, we have to face what it means to forgive others. Perhaps a way to start is by looking at what forgiveness is *not*. I think forgiveness is not a matter of the emotions. We are called upon to forgive precisely at the point where we feel most aggrieved or wounded, and to forgive those in whose presence we feel little delight. If we find it easy to forgive, then it is usually either because the offence did not injure us deeply or because it was given by one we delight in forgiving. So it is easy for me to forgive my children, even when they have driven me to distraction, because the desire for reconciliation with them is so strong, and the restoration of right relations such a pleasure.

Our feelings are much less helpful when we are confronted by someone with whom we have no natural affinity, towards whom we feel none of the attraction of friendship, with whom we would like nothing better than that we would never have to see them again, and with whom the prospect of right relations appeals like a plate of cold porridge. Our feelings are terribly changeable, prone to being swept about this way and that. At one moment we may feel loving and benign, often when other things are going well for us. In the next moment, something may happen which swings our mood; we are angry, fearful, hostile – and unforgiving. Our emotions are too tempestuous to be a reliable basis for forgiveness.

Nor is forgiveness a matter of the intellect. Mostly our sense of hurt comes from our perception that we have been unjustly treated, whether it be the offence of someone who did not understand how tired and weak we were, or of some individual or group who slighted us because we did not fit in, or simply the offence of life which has treated us unfairly, dealt us a bad hand, caused us to be lonely or unpopular or unsuccessful. We are called to forgive in situations where we believe that we are right and they are wrong; we have right on our side and they are mistaken. And though reason may help to clarify *why* we disagree, it will not often remove the disagreement. Nor will reason be the power which enables us to bridge the divide of disagreement or to suffer the pain of the injustice. To forgive, we also have to deal with our offended intellect, for forgiveness very often wars with our understanding of natural justice.

And though sheer willpower or force of decision may allow us to think more forgivingly, it will not protect us from the memories that come back to haunt us. We had not realised that seventy times seven could mean the *same* hurt as it replays itself over and over and over. Willpower may lift the burden from our consciences, but it will not heal our hurts or our hearts. Indeed, if our forgiveness is *only* an act of will, the effort of imposing it on ourselves may be damaging, and increase our awful sense of failure. How can we live with the clear call to forgive when all the while our human nature resists? How do we deal with the agony of the deceptive heart?

The problem about all of these – emotions, intellect, will – is that they leave the wrong relationship essentially unchanged. They operate only within *my* consciousness, and do not touch the other. They may describe more or less my intention, my hope, my motivation. They do not describe my *action*, and only my action changes things. Forgiveness is an action in which something changes, even just a little bit.

Rowan Williams, in a way I've found very helpful, describes forgiveness as a movement of turning. Forgiveness is turning to face our oppressor, the one who condemns, excludes, violates, injures us. Repentance is also a turning, to face the one we have condemned, excluded, violated or injured, our victim.

In Jesus Christ, we see that God identifies with the victim, with the condemned, excluded, violated, injured, not because they are pure or good or morally worthy or injured in a good cause, but simply *because* they are the victim. Not the good and respectable, not the righteous, not the deserving poor but *all* the poor, all who are excluded, judged, condemned. Criminals, drunkards, thieves – it is by virtue of their exclusion that God identifies with them, not because they are good but because they are human.

By all conventional worldly standards of right and wrong, Christianity is morally reprehensible. But then, it's not about morality, it's about salvation. We so easily forget that Christ Jesus came into the world to save sinners. We also forget that Jesus asked, 'Who among you is without sin?' And yet if we forget that, we make the reality of forgiveness an impossibility, and nowhere more so than in the task of forgiving ourselves, of accepting our acceptance.

Because this identification of God in Christ with the excluded, the victim, is very different from simply saying, *I will love you in spite of your faults and we won't think about them any more and we'll just pretend nothing has changed.* God is not with the victim to make us all victims. This is not a reversal to put the oppressor in turn in the place of victim. This is an invitation to go beyond the old categories of judge and sinner, of victim and oppressor into a new released relationship. It is an invitation to face our flaws, our failures, our weaknesses, our sins, and see precisely in them our hope. As Rowan Williams says, *'The Resurrection is an invitation to recognise one's victim as one's hope. Grace is released only in confrontation with one's victim.'*

In personal terms, I think this means turning to face those parts of ourselves which we most condemn, exclude, violate and victimise, recognising that not because we are virtuous or justified but because we are human, even these parts are accepted by God. And in fact, these are actually the parts of us God loves most, because they bear within them the possibility of the greatest transformation. Remember the woman who anointed Jesus. She loved much, because she had been forgiven much. Remember Peter, whose courage in the leadership of the first church sprang from the forgiveness of his cowardice, and Paul, whose passion for the gospel blossomed on the ashes of his equally passionate opposition to it.

So perhaps we can suggest that forgiving ourselves is an activity, a movement, a journey which has three stages. First there is a remembrance, an honest naming and recognition of wounds and hurts we have caused, a letting-go of denial or of endless self-justification. Then there is the turning to face all that we hate in and about ourselves, and accepting it as part of who we are. Like Orestes in the great classical Greek drama, we turn to face the Furies that pursue us and we take responsibility for our own actions. Until we do this, the Furies will pursue us relentlessly, however we try to escape them. And by the grace of God, we discover that in turning, the final word is not judgement but forgiveness, not condemnation but love. We are loved, even in our weakness and failure. The word of God, which is the word of life, is that we are forgiven people. We are set free to embrace even that which we found abhorrent and find in it the possibility of change and transformation. When Orestes embraced the Furies, they lost their power to tyrannise and became instead the Eumenides, the graces which set him on a new way of life. When the prodigal son turned and headed for home, he found welcome and forgiveness and love. We all have a prodigal son part of us. And this too is loved.

I believe in the forgiveness of sins ...

Not thought.
Its logic is remorselessly impotent.

Not feeling.
There are too many of them in an hour.

Not wish.
My desire eats itself.

Not instinct.
It locks into my bones.

Only action.

After an action, everything is changed,
Including me.
After an action, there is movement.
Thought, feeling, will, instinct, are different,
Even if only a little.
The ground has shifted.
Now,
What is the necessary action?

The Courage to Change

★

Here are three things I would like to show you. The first is a map of the world. Unfortunately, though it's only four years old, it's already out of date; there are countries named on it that no longer exist, such as Zaire, and others unnamed which do exist. Furthermore, there are botanical, geological and climatic alterations which, even on a different kind of map, probably wouldn't show up either – huge areas of forest gone, coastlines eroded, little islets drowned. The map of the earth has changed.

And here's a tin of baked beans, almost a staple of the British diet. It's not marked 'genetically modified', but it does contain modified maize starch, so there's a possibility that at some point on its journey to our tables, it too has been changed to contain more than just the humble bean of its appearance.

And the third is a picture of my three children. It's only a few years since it was taken, but all three of them have changed greatly from the photograph, and so has almost everything about their lives.

I share these familiar yet strange things with you to illustrate the unassailable fact of *change*. Because in reality, change is our only constant. It is the one thing we can be sure of – that things change. The whole fabric of the universe is in the process of change at every point. You and I, by the time we are forty, have not one single cell in our bodies that we had when we were ten years old. In the words of George MacLeod, *'All, all is in flux.'*

There are some changes that are so familiar to us that we come to think of them as *unchanging*: the movement of the earth around the sun and the passage of night and day; the progress of the seasons and the sustenance they deliver to us in the routines of planting and harvesting; the passing of the generations in birth and reproduction and death and regeneration. These are the changes of return, and we are confident enough of them to trust their stability. The cycles of life seem unchanging. Though my children grow and change, this is expected, this is the way it should be. Even though their changing brings about change for me, there are guidelines, precedents, traditions which I can draw on to help me adjust to these changes.

But for people living now, at the end of this millennium, change has implications beyond the ebb and flow, the patterns and rhythms of human existence. There have always been the crises and catastrophes that disrupted the rhythms, that tore the patterns apart – the tyrannies and wars and genocides, the imperial and colonial aggressions, the revolutions and counter-revolutions, the plagues and epidemics, the natural disasters and scarcities. There have been, too, the discoveries and adventures of the intellect and the imagination and the will and the spirit that have brought about change in the fabric of people's lives: the birth of great religious and political ideals and creative insights, the scientific dreams and discoveries, the renaissances and enlightenments, the exoduses and exiles and long marches, and in all of these, the coming of the new.

And there have been all of these in this century alone. The slow and painful task of reconstructing what has been deconstructed, of healing what has been broken, of reweaving the patterns, which has always been the human instinct, is far from complete even from the world war which ended more than fifty years ago, and its legacy is still with us in a dozen ways; the Balkans and the Middle East are only the most obvious examples. The history of the 20th century has been one of ceaseless change.

But now, on the threshold of a new century and a new millennium, we are in the throes of unprecedented change. The familiar disruptions and upheavals are still with us – only now they happen at a vastly accelerated pace, and on a scale magnified beyond our capacity to comprehend. Uprooted and migrant peoples now run into the tens of millions. Epidemics have become pandemics. Armaments easily possess the capacity to destroy the earth many times over, and to travel huge distances into space to do so. The world's dominant economic system can move money equivalent to the GNP of whole countries in a matter of seconds, and in casually so doing, the impact is felt in hundreds of places, by Iowa farmers and Korean engineers, by Swiss bankers and Malaysian rubber-tappers. Culture, education, philosophy, human institutions are all in rapid transition. Not only the scale and pace of change is new; the interconnectedness of it is also new. Because of economics, because of technology and the information explosion, because we are all globalised now, whether we know it or not, whether we like it or not, we are affected by changes that originate far from us, and of which we are simply collateral damage – and of course the changes that occur on our behalf affect others far from us equally. *'All, all is in flux; turn but a stone and an angel moves'* (G F MacLeod).

And as if this magnitude of change was not enough, there are changes taking place which seem to threaten not just our generations, not just those to come but the whole fabric of life on planet earth. In the last 25 years alone, human beings have destroyed one-third of our natural habitat, one-third of our non-renewable resources. We are already seeing the effects of ecological devastation across the globe; they are well documented. And beyond all of that, the nature of matter itself is facing potential change. Genetic engineering, cloning, all of the things that were once the stuff of science fiction seem to be coming closer, raising huge questions, fears and uncertainties. We live in a time of change which has no precedent.

Living as we do in a relatively stable country, it's easy to feel somewhat removed from the convulsions that are shaking the world. We, most of us, don't live in the eye of the storm, though we may feel its ripples in debates about genetically modified foods, or when job security is threatened or when interest rates rise or fall. Mostly, we don't bear the brunt of it; nevertheless, we are involved in it. In fact, we belong to the section of the earth's population which has, by and large, benefited from the changes. Our relatives have the open-heart surgery; our mobility is increased by travel; our children surf the net and access whole other worlds. We participate in change, knowingly or unknowingly.

If massive and continuous change to the world we inhabit and experience is actually the norm rather than the exception, which I think it is, what does it mean to face it? One of the commonest responses to sudden and dramatic change is shock. We are familiar with it from the victims of natural and human disasters, the earthquakes and hurricanes, the Hillsboroughs. The shock brings about a kind of paralysis, an apatheia, an apathy or lethargy in which action is impossible. But this is also a common response of people when confronted with the huge political or economic changes which translate at the personal level into such things as redundancy, bankruptcy, 24-hour working patterns or other kind of major upheaval. It may be accompanied by other feelings, by depression, even despair, by guilt at survival or complicity, by denial and a curious attempt to carry on as if nothing has happened.

Perhaps there is an extent to which we all participate to a degree in these kinds of responses. They stem from a perception of extreme powerlessness, from the feeling of losing control over our own bit of the world, however limited that may be and of being disabled from doing anything to stop it or redress it. Perhaps the underlying question we are seeking to address here is one, not of change but of counterchange. How can we be agents of change not just its unwilling or compromised recipients? How can we engage with the changes that are going on around us in a creative way? What kind of people do we need to be and how do we become them, to be agents of change for the good – and how do we determine what the good is anyway? And how, in the midst of all that grappling with change, all that information, all these choices, do we not die of anxiety?

And does our spirituality help us to respond creatively to change around us? Does it enable us to undergo the painful changes in our own lives needed to make these responses? Is it the kind of secure home from which we can embrace the challenge and adventure of going out into an uncertain and complex world?

Following Jesus in the footsteps of the disciples

I emphasise a spirituality for change because it seems to me to be one of the clearest characteristics of a significant group of people for all Christians.

It is from the disciples that we learn all that we know about Jesus. The gospels are as much their story as the story of Jesus. It is not Jesus who tells us of his own life and death and resurrection, nor is it either the common people nor the leaders of the society. We see the whole thing through their eyes.

The life that they shared with him that was the basis of the training they received is the starting point for our discipleship today. Our questions go back to their experience. *They learned by doing*, and then by reflecting on what they had learned. Much of that reflection took the form of questions – the questions they asked of Jesus, but even more, the questions he asked of them.

And their life together was very much a journey. Not only were they almost always on the move, travelling around the country and gradually moving closer to their final destination in Jerusalem. They were also on an inner journey, towards greater understanding, maturity, faith. They were growing in discipleship. They played an essential part in everything that Jesus did, and it is clear that their training was a major focus of his life and ministry. Because they had lived the life of the Kingdom with Jesus, they in their turn could invite others to live that life too.

The part the disciples played in Jesus' life and ministry was not just as individuals but as a body. They were the community of faith he was building.

Their calling as disciples had profound implications. They found themselves beside him having to:

- take a public stand; expose their faith, their hopes and their failures out in the open;
- live a life of corporate activity and obedience;
- be active not passive; they could not be withdrawn and ascetic like the followers of John the Baptist, nor could they be scholars and theorists like the Pharisees; they learned as they lived;
- mix in strange, sometimes disreputable company.

The disciples had many struggles with all of this. Some of them thought Jesus could have had a better programme. Some of them thought he allowed too many interruptions. There was much they didn't understand. But as they came to understand more, to see in Jesus' way, he expected them to share more and more in his ministry. And as their loyalty and commitment as a group became stronger, they were given individual tasks. Their personal commitment was deepened and nurtured by Jesus, and he constantly reminded them that they had been called not because they were more faithful or morally superior but because he had a job for them to do.

This journey with Jesus was not a training in religion but a *training in life*, and not a different life, but the same life lived in a different way – a freer, more fulfilling way, in which he was teaching them the greatness of humility, and of meeting others not as strangers but as friends.

It is clear from the gospels that almost everything that happened from the time Jesus appeared in their lives constituted huge and shattering change. His call changed their view of their society, their religion, their relationships, their self-understanding, their way of life. This change was not easy for them: they struggled; they doubted; and it's patently obvious that half the time they didn't have a clue what was going on, how they should interpret it or how they should respond. Every single familiar marker disappeared, bit by bit, till that final point after the crucifixion where they huddled and hid as a devastated and broken band of people, bereft not only of all the old certainties but of the new relationship too, beaten, ashamed, lost and terrified. But in their life together with Jesus, gradually a new spirituality had been shaping, a spirituality for change and transformation that made them able to trust in the resurrection when it came.

I think there are a number of characteristics of that spirituality that we can look to as being enabling of change for us.

It was marked by movement. These were people who walked, kept moving, didn't have much opportunity to hang about studying the state of their souls.

It was marked by being very close to the life of their community; it was crowded with people who were suffering, angry, oppressed, excluded; I mean physically as well as spiritually crowded. As such, it was often untidy, chaotic and frightening.

It was marked by profound questioning; not only their own doubtful and confused questioning of Jesus, but also by his questioning of them, making them take stands, articulate a response at a level that went beyond both intellect and feeling into sheer intuition and decision.

It was marked by corporateness, by belonging to a community of people who did not always like each other, agree with each other or trust each other, and whose numbers were continually being added to by more people they didn't approve of, but who had to just get on with it if they wanted to stay on the road with Jesus.

It was marked above all by singular and intense personal attachment to Jesus. There is little sense of the disciples following him because of some great intellectual or moral conviction. They went because he asked them, and because they loved to be with him. And through all of their vicissitudes on the way, that sense of having their 'eyes on the prize' of Jesus and his different way of seeing never really left them.

And as for the things that could block change, could resist it, could even kill to prevent it, well, the disciples saw how these showed up as well, and when they missed seeing, Jesus pointed it out to them.

There were the people who were like Lot's wife, who couldn't change because they were paralysed by their attachment to the past, who, just when they most needed to keep going forward, would stop and look back, and would, for all the world like a pillar of salt, get stuck, immobilised, whether by grief or shame, by the longing for past achievements and experiences, or simply by the inability to let go and move on.

There were the people who were like the rich ruler who couldn't change because they were too weighed down by stuff, who simply were too scared of losing what they had to be able to ditch it and learn to travel light. But as the disciples had learned, you had to be ready to travel light.

There were the people who didn't want to be healed, who couldn't answer that question that Jesus asked the blind man by the temple gate because actually they saw that being healed – changing – meant taking responsibility for your life, and not being a victim any more, and that it would all involve an awful lot of hard work.

There were the people who were too attached to their own particular picture of themselves, like Jesus' own townspeople, who couldn't change because they didn't like it when the critique was turned on them and who simply closed their minds to the possibility of something different.

There were the people like the tax-collector in the temple, who couldn't change because, actually, they didn't need to change; there was nothing wrong with them: it was everybody else who needed to change.

And then there were the people whose profit, power and influence would be threatened by change.

We've probably all been all of these at some time in our lives.

In all of these people, there was a fear in there somewhere. If anything blocks change, it's fear. I think it's not wicked or immoral or weak to feel fear. It's just human. The disciples felt fear a lot; Jesus felt fear. But for them, they had something that was even stronger than fear that helped them to take the risks of change, to take the leap into the unknown, the new. They all, including Jesus, who was fabulously open to change, kept their eyes on the prize.

The things that have enabled the disciples to change are not different from those things that have enabled change in countless others. That, I think, is because the good news they got from Jesus was not about being religious, it was about being human. It's a thing that I am more and more aware of as I get older, and see more of the world, just how extraordinary is the human capacity for change, for adapting to the most difficult of circumstances and still remaining creative and hopeful.

Perhaps hope is the key that most unlocks the doors of change for us. It was hope that Jesus offered to people who were fearful, stuck, marginalised, that he awakened in his companions, that allowed him to create a community open to the utterly new and strange fact of resurrection. As we stand confronting change that is new and strange beyond our comprehension, what is the living hope that *we* have as a community to make of the welter a world that will last, to make transformation possible?